Future-Proof

A Strategic Guide to Keeping Your Job, Growing Your Value, and Becoming Indispensable in the AI Workplace

Ryan Brooks

ISBN 979-8-9996566-0-5

Contents

Introduction: AI Is Not Coming; It's Already Here

The email that effectively ended her career arrived on a Tuesday. For one UK-based copywriter, it was the confirmation of a verdict she had already overheard just days before. After years of building a successful freelance career, her main client, a major international brand, was terminating her contract. The reason? They could now get the work done faster and cheaper. The new hire was not a rival freelancer or a hotshot agency; it was an algorithm. "One day, I overheard my boss saying to a colleague, 'Just put it in ChatGPT,'" she recalled. Shortly after, she was gone. The work that had once required her skill, nuance, and understanding of brand voice was now just another prompt, a task to be executed by a machine. "AI scares the hell out of me," she confessed, her personal shock echoing a broader professional anxiety. "I feel devastated for the younger generation, it's taking all the creative jobs."[1]

Across the continent in Poland, a popular radio presenter discovered his voice and persona had been cloned into an AI-powered avatar, designed to host a show 24/7 without a break. He and several colleagues were let go, their years of experience and connection with listeners deemed replaceable by a synthetic replica. Public outrage eventually forced the station to pull the plug on the experiment, but the presenter's warning lingered. Artificial intelligence, he noted, "can't replace our curiosity, creativity or emotional intelligence."[2] His point was sharp and clear: the technology could mimic the output, but it could not replicate the human spirit that created it.

This erosion of creative value is a story playing out globally. In Indonesia, a talented illustrator watched in dismay as her commissions for album art and book covers evaporated. "Since AI took off, my workload has plummeted," she explained, noting a drop from around fifteen commissions a month to just five.[3] Clients who once valued her unique artistic vision were now feeding her past drawings into generative AI tools like Midjourney to produce new images. Even the government, a former source of work, had begun using AI art instead of hiring human creators. The economic impact was immediate and punishing. "Even those who've kept their jobs have had their wages reduced," she observed, as companies adopted AI for design tasks, turning a skilled craft into a commodity.[4]

These are not cautionary tales from a distant, dystopian future. They are the lived realities of professionals right now. The age of artificial intelligence is not a far-off event to prepare for; it is a present-day reality that is actively reshaping careers, industries, and economies. The machine colleague has arrived, and it is already taking on tasks from writing marketing copy and drafting legal documents to analyzing financial data and even generating its own code.

This disruption is fueling a pervasive and understandable anxiety, one that is amplified by a constant drumbeat of dire predictions from the very top of the corporate world. This is the view from the C-suite, and it is unsettling. Ford's CEO, Jim Farley, stated bluntly that "artificial intelligence is going to replace literally half of all white-collar workers in the U.S."[5] Dario Amodei, the head of the prominent AI lab Anthropic, warned that AI could wipe out half of all entry-level white-collar jobs within five years.[6] At a conference for finance professionals, private equity billionaire Robert F. Smith predicted that within a year, "40% of the people at this conference will have an AI agent and the remaining 60% will be looking for work."[7]

These are not just abstract forecasts; they are being backed by action. At JPMorgan Chase, an executive told investors that AI would enable the bank to reduce headcount by 10% in its operations departments.[8] IBM's CEO, Arvind Krishna, confirmed that his company had already used AI to automate hundreds of roles in its own human resources department.[9] The message has been reinforced by a wave of hiring freezes and policy changes. Salesforce CEO Marc Benioff publicly mused, "Maybe we aren't going to hire anybody this year," specifically regarding engineering roles.[10] At Shopify, CEO Tobi Lütke issued a memo instructing managers to prove that AI could not do a job before requesting to hire a new person.[11] The message from the top seems clear: a great displacement is underway, driven by a relentless push for efficiency.

But this is not the whole story. While some doors are closing, others are opening for those who know where to look. A 28-year-old graphic designer was shocked when his six-year job was eliminated because, as he put it, "much of my work was being replaced by AI." His story, shared in a viral video, drew hundreds of similar accounts from professionals feeling the same pressure.[12] Yet his story did not end there. He eventually landed a new role in content creation at a firm that explicitly "doesn't agree with replacing human roles with AI," using the technology only to assist, never to fully generate creative content.[13] His experience reveals a crucial truth: the impact of AI is not uniform. It is a choice made by organizations and individuals.

This book is not about stoking fear. It is about replacing that fear with a plan. It is about showing you how to navigate this new landscape and find your place in a world where human and machine intelligence work together.

The narrative of mass replacement overlooks a more nuanced and, ultimately, more empowering reality. The real threat is not the technology itself, but being unprepared for it. A groundbreaking 2024 study from Stanford University's Institute for Human-Centered AI (HAI) reframes the entire debate. After surveying thousands of workers across more than one hundred occupations, the researchers discovered something profound. Workers do not want AI to take over their jobs. They want to partner with it. The overwhelming desire, expressed by a clear majority, is to automate the "drudgery", the repetitive, tedious, and low-value tasks, in order to free themselves up for more meaningful, creative, and high-impact work.[14]

This insight is the key to understanding the entire AI revolution in the workplace. It is not a battle of human versus machine, but a negotiation over the nature of work itself. People are not inherently anti-technology; they are anti-drudgery. They are seeking ways to offload the parts of their jobs that drain their energy and creativity, so they can focus on the parts they find fulfilling.

This desire is vividly illustrated by the story of Walton Goggins, an Emmy-nominated actor with a creative idea but no business background. He wanted to launch a line of unique eyewear, but as he admitted, he was "short on time and knowledge of how to start a business" and had "no idea what I'm doing" in that domain.[15] His vision was stalled by the exact kind of administrative drudgery that the Stanford study identified.

In 2024, he partnered with the web services company GoDaddy to see if AI could bridge that gap. The company's AI platform handled the operational grind: it designed a logo, built a functional e-commerce website, generated a social media marketing calendar, and automated customer confirmation emails. This freed Goggins to focus on his creative vision. The result? The business received its first order within an hour of launching and was soon featured in major publications like GQ and The Hollywood Reporter.[16]

The Goggins story is a powerful counterpoint to the tales of displacement. It shows AI not as a replacement for human creativity, but as an engine for it. It is a microcosm of a larger trend. A 2025 survey of small business owners found that 72% of those using AI tools reported increased productivity, while 61% saw higher revenues.[17] AI is becoming a great democratizer of opportunity, allowing individuals and small teams to compete by automating the operational burdens that once required significant capital and staff.

This reveals the two mindsets that will define the future of careers.

On one side is AI Anxiety: the fear of being replaced, the worry that your skills are becoming obsolete, and the feeling of being powerless against a relentless wave of automation. This is the experience of the copywriter who sees her craft devalued and the illustrator whose commissions disappear. It is a defensive crouch, a reaction to a threat that feels overwhelming. This anxiety is widespread; a 2024 Pew Research study found that 52% of all U.S. workers are concerned about AI's potential effects in the workplace.[18] It is a mindset rooted in the fear of obsolescence.

On the other is the AI Advantage: the strategic decision to augment your abilities with technology, to automate the mundane, and to double down on the uniquely human skills that machines cannot replicate. It is a mindset of collaboration, not competition. This is the mindset of the entrepreneur who uses AI to handle logistics so he can focus on his product, or the professional who leverages AI to become more productive and valuable in her role.

The evidence for this advantage is already emerging. A 2023 survey found that 38% of workers who use ChatGPT reported getting a pay raise, with many attributing it to increased productivity and the ability to take on more complex tasks.[19] They were not being rewarded for being replaced; they were being rewarded for using AI to become better at their jobs.

This book is your playbook for cultivating the AI Advantage. It is built on a clear, three-part framework designed to give you control over your career narrative in an age of disruption.

1. Adapt Faster. The first pillar is about understanding the new landscape. The pace of change is accelerating, and standing still is no longer an option. In a world where the required skills for AI-exposed jobs are changing 66% faster than for other jobs, adaptability is the new currency of career security.[20] Adapting faster means developing the awareness to see where technology is heading and how it intersects with your industry and role. It involves honestly assessing which parts of your job are vulnerable to automation, the routine, the predictable, the data-driven, and identifying the areas where you can provide unique, human value. This is not about becoming a technical expert overnight; it is about becoming a strategic realist

who can anticipate shifts and position yourself ahead of the curve.

2. Stay Human. The second pillar is your offensive strategy. As machines become more capable of handling analytical and repetitive tasks, our uniquely human qualities become our greatest competitive advantage. This is your "Human Edge." This book will introduce a memorable model for understanding these skills: Creativity, Humanity, Adaptability, and Thinking (C.H.A.T.). These are the domains where AI still struggles: genuine ideation, deep empathy and interpersonal connection, resilient navigation of ambiguity, and the application of ethical judgment and critical thought. Cultivating these skills is not a soft platitude; it is a hard-nosed career strategy to ensure you are doing work that machines cannot. As one executive at USAA noted, her company's strategy is shifting to focus on skills that are "uniquely human (and moving away from skills that machines can master)."[21]

3. Use AI Better. The third pillar is about execution. It is no longer enough to be aware of AI; you must become proficient in using it. This pillar is about moving from being a casual, passive user to a power user who actively directs AI as a tool. This means going beyond asking an AI to write an email and learning to use it as a personal tutor to get up to speed in a new role, as a research assistant to synthesize vast amounts of information, and as a creative partner to brainstorm and challenge your own ideas. A landmark Harvard study found that professionals who integrated AI into their workflow were not only 25% faster but also produced work of 40% higher quality.[22]

Mastering this skill means you are not just a human competing with AI, but a human augmented by AI: a combination that is far more powerful than either one alone.

Think of this book as a strategic guide, a practical playbook for navigating the most significant workplace transformation of our lifetime. It is not a technical manual filled with jargon, but a career roadmap written in clear, actionable language. It is divided into parts tailored to your specific needs, whether you are a student choosing a major and wondering which fields are safe, an early-career professional trying to build a standout portfolio, or a mid-career professional feeling the ground shift beneath your feet and looking for a way to pivot without panic.

We will move from understanding the threat to mastering the opportunity. We will explore which career paths offer the most resilience and how to "armor up" your skills for the future. We will provide tactical advice for hacking the new AI-driven hiring systems and for integrating AI into your daily work from day one.

The goal is to empower you. The future of work is not something that happens to you; it is something you can actively shape. The 28-year-old graphic designer who lost his job to an algorithm and then found a better one offered the most succinct advice for this new era. It is a call to action for every professional who wants to move from anxiety to advantage.

"Learn as many skills as possible," he urged. "You have to be prepared."[23]

This book will show you how.

PART I: UNDERSTAND THE THREAT AND THE OPPORTUNITY

Chapter 1: The Machine Colleague Has Arrived

Introduction

The realization that your job is at risk often comes not as a formal announcement, but as a quiet, chilling discovery. For a 28-year-old graphic designer, it came in the form of a slow, creeping obsolescence. After six years at his company, he noticed the demand for his skills was waning. The projects that once required his creative eye and technical proficiency were increasingly being handled by new, automated systems. The company was not just experimenting with artificial intelligence; it was integrating it into the core of its creative workflow. His role, once central to the team, was being systematically replaced by an algorithm. The shock of his eventual layoff was compounded by a sense of bewilderment. His job had not been outsourced to a cheaper market or given to a junior employee; it had been absorbed by a machine.[24]

This designer's story is a potent illustration of a new reality unfolding across the professional landscape. The machine colleague has arrived. It does not need a desk, a parking space, or a benefits package, but it is rapidly becoming a fixture in offices everywhere. This is not a distant forecast; it is a systemic integration that is happening now. AI is fundamentally altering the nature of work in industries from finance and law to marketing and education. This change feels different from past technological shifts. It is not about a new machine on a factory floor or a new piece of software to be mastered. It is about a new form of intelligence entering the workplace, one that can perform cognitive tasks that were, until very recently, the exclusive domain of human knowledge workers.

This chapter will show how this integration is taking place and provide the foundational concepts you need to navigate it. To build a resilient career in this new era, you must first understand the language of this disruption and the two powerful, divergent paths it is creating for the future of work.

Automation vs. Augmentation: A Tale of Two Futures

The terms "automation" and "augmentation" are often used interchangeably in conversations about AI, but they represent two vastly different futures. Understanding the distinction is the first step toward building a strategic response.

Automation is when a machine replaces a human task entirely. It is a story of substitution, where technology is deployed to perform a function more efficiently or cheaply than a person can. It is the path of pure efficiency, and its logic is compellingly simple.

A stark and powerful example comes from the Swedish financial technology company Klarna. In early 2024, the company announced that its new AI-powered customer service assistant was a staggering success. In its first month of operation, the AI handled 2.3 million conversations, accounting for two-thirds of all the company's customer service chats. It performed the equivalent work of 700 full-time human agents. The AI was not only efficient but also effective, boasting a similar customer satisfaction score to its human counterparts while resolving issues in an average of two minutes. It took eleven minutes for a human agent. The financial implications were enormous, with the company projecting an annual profit increase of $40 million as a direct result of this single implementation.[25]

This is a clear and unambiguous case of automation. A specific, repeatable job function, first-line customer support, was transferred from a large team of humans to a single, scalable AI system. The goal was substitution, and the result was a dramatic reduction in the need for human labor for that specific task. For the 700 people whose work was effectively absorbed by the AI, this was not a story of empowerment. It was a story of displacement.

Augmentation, on the other hand, is when a machine assists a human, enhancing their abilities rather than replacing them. It is a story of collaboration, where technology acts as a tool to amplify human expertise. The most prominent example of this model is Microsoft's Copilot, an AI assistant embedded across its entire suite of Office products. Copilot does not replace the financial analyst, the marketing manager, or the project lead. Instead, it acts as a partner, a tireless assistant working alongside the professional.[26]

To understand augmentation in practice, consider a day in the life of a marketing manager. She begins her morning not with a blank page, but with a conversation. She asks Copilot to analyze the previous week's campaign data and identify the top three performing audience segments. In seconds, the AI processes the data and provides a summary, a task that might have previously taken an hour of filtering spreadsheets. Next, she needs to create a presentation for leadership about a new product launch. Instead of spending hours designing slides, she gives Copilot a simple prompt based on her project outline. The AI generates a complete, professional-looking presentation, complete with relevant images and speaker notes. She then spends her time refining the strategic message and tailoring the narrative, rather than wrestling with formatting. Later, she needs to draft an email to her team outlining the week's priorities. She tells Copilot the key points, and it generates a clear, well-structured draft, which she quickly edits for tone and nuance.

In this model, the human professional remains firmly in control. She sets the strategy, makes the final judgments, and provides the creative and ethical oversight. The AI acts as a powerful force multiplier, freeing her from lower-value work to focus on more complex challenges. The machine handles the mechanical data processing and content generation, while the human provides the wisdom, context, and strategic direction. The goal is not substitution, but a partnership that elevates the quality and impact of the human's work.

These two models, automation and augmentation, are not mutually exclusive (some roles will experience a blend of both) but they represent the fundamental choice facing every organization. Will AI be used primarily to replace people for cost savings, or to empower them for greater value creation?

The Human Response: Drudgery vs. Meaningful Work

The direction a company chooses is not solely a top-down decision. The success of any AI implementation depends heavily on the human response, and a landmark study from Stanford University's Institute for Human-Centered AI (HAI) provides the clearest insight yet into the psychology of AI adoption. The 2024 study, titled "What Workers Really Want from Artificial

Intelligence," reveals that workers are not irrationally afraid of technology; they are making a very logical and intuitive calculation about the kind of work they want to do.

The study found that professionals are most eager to offload tasks they consider "drudgery." This category includes the tedious, repetitive, and often thankless parts of a job: scheduling appointments across multiple time zones, correcting data entry errors, organizing vast amounts of information, and handling other routine administrative duties. These are the tasks that drain cognitive energy and get in the way of what employees perceive as their "real" work. For these activities, workers see AI as a welcome tool of liberation.

Conversely, the study found that these same workers are highly resistant to AI encroaching on tasks that are central to their professional identity and sense of fulfillment. They actively push back when AI threatens to take over work that requires creativity, high-level strategy, sensitive communication with clients, or mentoring junior colleagues. This is the line in the sand. When AI is perceived as a tool to eliminate drudgery, it is embraced. When it is perceived as a threat to meaningful work, it is resisted. This resistance is not just about fear of job loss; it is about protecting one's professional identity.

This framework explains the visceral, negative reactions of creative professionals to generative AI. When a U.S. voice actor discovered his client had used AI to clone his voice, generating new lines for projects without his permission or payment, it was a profound violation of his core craft.[27] A person's voice is a unique biometric signature, inextricably linked to their identity. For an actor, it is the primary instrument of their art and livelihood. The AI was not being used to automate his scheduling or invoicing; it was being used to replicate his unique talent, effectively stealing his professional essence.

Similarly, for the Indonesian illustrator whose unique style was fed into an AI to generate derivative works, the technology was not a helpful assistant; it was a competitor threatening the very source of her artistic and professional value. In these cases, AI crossed the line from automating drudgery to threatening the work that gives a career its meaning and purpose. It triggered a deep-seated professional identity threat, a fear that the skills and talents honed over years could be rendered worthless.

This distinction provides a clear roadmap for successful human-AI collaboration. The AI Advantage is found not in a race against the machine, but in a partnership with it. The goal for any professional should be to strategically automate their own drudgery, using AI as a lever to free up their time and cognitive energy to focus on the uniquely human, high-value work that machines cannot do. This is not a futuristic theory; it is a practical strategy being deployed right now in thousands of workplaces.

The Hybrid Workplace is Everywhere

The integration of AI into daily professional life is no longer confined to the tech industry. The machine colleague is showing up in every sector, creating hybrid human-AI workflows that are rapidly becoming the new standard.

In the legal profession, a field built on precedent and painstaking research, AI is making dramatic inroads. Before the rise of advanced AI, a junior associate at a major law firm could expect to spend thousands of hours on document review, manually sifting through mountains of contracts and communications to find relevant evidence. This work was a rite of passage, but it was also a form of high-stakes drudgery. Today, platforms like Harvey AI, which is built on OpenAI's advanced models, can perform this task in a fraction of the time. This does not eliminate the need for lawyers. Instead, it fundamentally changes their role. It allows a junior associate to move almost immediately to higher-value work: analyzing the patterns the AI has found, building a case strategy, and advising clients.

As Dr. Claudia Junker, the General Counsel for the German telecommunications giant Deutsche Telekom, explained, "Harvey is like a Swiss Army knife; it simplifies tasks such as document analysis, contract comparisons, drafting, and translations, freeing us to focus on strategic priorities."[28] The AI handles the laborious research, empowering the human expert to deliver more strategic value from day one.

In finance and accounting, a sector defined by numbers and analysis, AI adoption is accelerating. A Q2 2025 Gallup poll found that 32% of professionals in the finance industry now use AI frequently in their roles, making it one of the leading sectors for integration.[29] This means that nearly one in three of your colleagues in the field is already leveraging these tools regularly. This goes far beyond simple calculators. Tools like Microsoft Copilot for Excel are changing how analysts work, allowing them to use natural language prompts to clean data, generate pivot tables, and run complex scenario models. The AI performs the mechanical data manipulation that is prone to human error and consumes significant time, enabling the human analyst to spend more of their day on interpretation, strategic insight, and communicating those findings to stakeholders. The machine crunches the numbers; the human provides the wisdom.

This pattern of augmentation repeats across nearly every field of knowledge work. In software development, Microsoft CEO Satya Nadella noted that AI tools like GitHub Copilot are now writing up to 30% of new code, reducing the need for layers of support teams.[30] This does not mean developers are becoming obsolete. It means they can offload the task of writing boilerplate and repetitive code to the AI, allowing them to focus on more complex architectural challenges and creative problem-solving. In marketing and design, tools like Canva Magic Write are embedded directly into creative workflows. They can generate dozens of first-draft headlines for an ad campaign or initial copy for a website, which are then refined, edited, and approved by human marketers who oversee brand voice and strategy.[31]

In education, Khan Academy's AI tutor, Khanmigo, acts as a personalized learning assistant for students. It does not simply give them the answers. Instead, it uses a Socratic method of questioning to guide them through problems, helping them understand the underlying concepts. It provides one-on-one support outside of classroom hours, a resource previously available only to the wealthiest students. This frees the human teacher to focus on pedagogy, classroom management, and the social and emotional development of their students.[32] In countless offices, general-purpose tools like Notion AI are being used to summarize meeting notes, draft project plans, and organize team knowledge, absorbing the administrative overhead that has long been a source of workplace drudgery.[33]

Conclusion

The machine colleague is no longer a hypothetical concept from science fiction. It is a real and present feature of the modern workplace. Its integration is not a passing trend but a systemic shift that is reconfiguring roles and redefining value in every industry. As we have seen, this technology can manifest in two distinct ways: as an engine of automation that substitutes for human labor, or as a tool of augmentation that amplifies human expertise. The most successful and sustainable applications of AI are those that align with what workers themselves desire: the automation of drudgery to free up time for more meaningful, creative, and strategic work.

The arrival of the machine colleague is therefore not a signal to panic, but a prompt to analyze. The first and most important strategic move any professional can make is to look at their own role through this new lens. Take a moment to perform a simple audit of your own job. Make a list of your daily and weekly tasks, from the most mundane to the most complex. Now, divide that list into two columns.

In the first column, list the tasks that constitute "drudgery." Be honest and specific. Which parts of your job are repetitive, rule-based, and often feel like they get in the way of your "real" work? This might include filling out expense reports, scheduling meetings, manually compiling data for a weekly report, writing standard follow-up emails, or answering the same five customer questions over and over again. These are the tasks that are most vulnerable to automation, and you should view that vulnerability not as a threat, but as an opportunity for liberation.

In the second column, list the tasks that constitute "meaningful work." These are the parts of your job that require your unique skills, judgment, and creativity. This is the work that energizes you and where you feel you create the most value. It might include negotiating a complex deal with a new client, mentoring a junior team member, brainstorming a novel solution to a persistent problem, resolving a delicate interpersonal conflict, or using your intuition and experience to make a difficult strategic decision when the data is ambiguous. These are the tasks that define your Human Edge.

This simple audit is the beginning of your future-proofing strategy. The tasks in the first column represent the parts of your job you should actively seek to automate or augment with AI. The tasks in the second column represent the areas where you should focus your professional development, doubling down on the skills that make you uniquely valuable. By proactively managing this balance, you shift from being a passive target of technological change to an active architect of your own career. The goal is not to out-compete the machine, but to collaborate with it, making yourself not just a worker, but an indispensable, AI-empowered professional.

This analysis is the foundation upon which all the other strategies in this book are built. Now that we have established how the machine colleague is arriving in the workplace, the next chapter will explore the fierce and conflicting debate among experts about what happens next, and how bad the disruption will really get.

Chapter 2: The Great Debate: How Bad Will It Really Get?

Introduction

In the summer of 2025, influential thinkers gathered at the Aspen Ideas Festival in the idyllic setting of Aspen, Colorado. Ford Motor Company's CEO, Jim Farley, delivered a forecast that sent a shockwave through the professional world. With the casual certainty of a man stating a simple fact, he predicted that "artificial intelligence is going to replace literally half of all white-collar workers in the U.S."[34] The statement was not couched in academic jargon or softened with corporate platitudes. It was a stark, numerical prediction of a massive societal upheaval, delivered by the leader of one of America's most iconic companies. What made the comment so potent was its source. This was not a Silicon Valley futurist or an AI evangelist talking up their own technology; this was the head of a legacy industrial giant, a company at the heart of the American economy, publicly forecasting a hollowing out of the professional class.

Farley's comment was not an outlier; it was the public articulation of a conversation that is happening in boardrooms and on earnings calls across the globe. It represents one side of the great debate that is defining the future of work, a debate that pits dire warnings of mass displacement against optimistic visions of a new era of human-machine collaboration. This is arguably the most important economic and social question of our time, and the experts are deeply and fundamentally divided. On one side, there is a growing chorus of voices arguing that "this time is different," that the cognitive capabilities of AI represent a form of automation so profound that it will break the historical pattern of technological progress, leading to widespread and permanent job losses. On the other side, economists and technologists argue that AI, like the steam engine or the computer before it, is a powerful new tool that will ultimately augment human capability, destroy old jobs but create new ones, and usher in an era of unprecedented productivity and growth.

This chapter will take you inside that debate. We will stand before the "Forecast Wall," examining the mounting evidence for widespread disruption, not as abstract predictions but as concrete corporate strategies. We will then explore the powerful counter-arguments, grounded in economic history and sophisticated theory, that suggest a more hopeful path is not only possible, but likely. By understanding why the experts are so deeply divided (the different time horizons they operate on, the vested interests that shape their views, and the critical distinction between automating a task and eliminating a job) you will see that the future is not a fixed destination to be predicted, but a contested territory that is still being shaped.

Section 1: The Forecast Wall: The Case for Disruption

The anxiety that many professionals feel is not an overreaction; it is a direct response to a steady stream of alarming forecasts and actions from some of the most powerful figures in technology and business. This is the evidence for disruption, a forecast wall built brick by brick from public statements, internal memos, and real-world job cuts. It is a compelling and coherent case for a future of significant displacement.

The predictions for job loss are often breathtaking in their scale and specificity. Dario Amodei, the CEO of the influential AI lab Anthropic, projected that AI could eliminate half of all entry-level white-collar jobs in the United States within the next one to five years, potentially spiking unemployment to between 10 and 20 percent.[35] His forecast is particularly chilling because it targets the most vulnerable segment of the professional workforce: those just starting their careers.

These entry-level roles, the junior analyst, the paralegal, the marketing coordinator, have traditionally served as the training ground for the next generation of leaders. They are where young professionals learn the ropes, build their networks, and develop the foundational skills for a long career. These jobs are often composed of well-defined, task-based work, such as summarizing documents, compiling data, or writing basic reports, making them prime candidates for automation by generative AI. Amodei's prediction suggests a future where the first rung on the corporate ladder is sawed off, leaving a generation of graduates with nowhere to begin and creating a long-term talent pipeline problem for companies that will one day need experienced leaders.

This sentiment is echoed in industry-specific warnings that target even seasoned professionals. At a 2025 conference packed with finance professionals, the private equity billionaire Robert F. Smith offered an even more immediate and personal warning. Looking out at the crowd of highly paid experts, he predicted that within a single year, "40% of the people at this conference will have an AI agent and the remaining 60% will be looking for work."[36] The implication was clear: in a data-driven field like finance, the analytical power of AI would create a sharp divide between those who leverage the technology and those who are rendered obsolete by it. It was a brutal assessment of the speed at which AI could reorder the hierarchy of a sophisticated, high-stakes industry, suggesting that years of experience would be no protection against this new wave of automation.

These are not just abstract numbers; they are being translated into concrete actions that are already affecting workers. These are not future predictions, but present-day realities. At IBM, a legacy technology company navigating its own transformation, CEO Arvind Krishna confirmed in May 2025 that the company had already used AI to automate and eliminate "a couple hundred" roles within its own corporate human resources department.[37] The functions being replaced were not peripheral tasks, but core HR responsibilities like processing employment verification letters and moving employees between departments. It was a clear signal that the administrative backbone of the modern corporation is a key target for automation. If a company like IBM is willing to automate its own internal people-management functions, it sends a powerful message about the perceived efficiency gains of replacing human administrative work with AI.

At Microsoft, the company at the forefront of deploying generative AI to the public, CEO Satya Nadella revealed that AI tools like GitHub Copilot were already writing up to 30 percent of new code. This dramatic increase in productivity allowed the company to reduce the need for layers of software development support teams, as the AI could handle many of the routine queries and coding tasks that once required human intervention.[38] In the financial sector, JPMorgan Chase's consumer banking chief, Marianne Lake, announced to investors that AI would enable the bank to reduce its headcount by 10 percent in its operations and account services departments, a move that could affect thousands of employees.[39] This was not a vague forecast, but a specific target announced to the financial markets, indicating a firm corporate commitment to achieving cost savings through AI-driven headcount reduction.

This trend of displacement is further reinforced by a strategic shift in hiring practices at some of the world's most influential companies. The message being sent to managers and the market is clear: before we hire a human, we must first see if an AI can do the job. This represents a fundamental change in the philosophy of corporate growth. In early 2025, Salesforce CEO Marc Benioff publicly mused, "Maybe we aren't going to hire anybody this year," specifically regarding engineering roles, suggesting that existing teams could become vastly more productive by leveraging AI tools.[40]

In an internal memo that quickly became public, Shopify's CEO, Tobi Lütke, made this an explicit policy. He instructed his managers that they "must demonstrate why they cannot get what they want done using AI" before any request for new headcount would be approved.[41] This is a profound reordering of priorities. The default assumption is no longer that growth requires more people; the default assumption is that growth should first be powered by technology.

Human hiring is becoming the option of last resort, a step to be taken only after the limits of automation have been reached. This shifts the burden of proof onto managers to justify human roles in a world where AI is seen as the primary engine of productivity. Amazon's CEO, Andy Jassy, echoed this sentiment in his own internal memo, stating that AI-driven efficiencies would mean the company "will need fewer people doing some of the jobs that are being done today."[42]

These statements, taken together, paint a deeply unsettling picture. They suggest a future where human labor is increasingly seen as a cost to be minimized, where efficiency is the ultimate corporate goal, and where AI is the primary tool for achieving it. This is the pessimistic view, and it is a powerful one. It is the narrative that fuels AI Anxiety, the fear that your skills, your experience, and your job are on a path to obsolescence.

Section 2: The Counter-Argument: A More Hopeful Path

While the forecast wall is imposing, it only tells one side of the story. A powerful set of counter-arguments, grounded in economic history, sophisticated theory, and a different reading of the data, suggests a far more optimistic future. This perspective does not deny the reality of disruption, but it reframes it as a process of transformation rather than simple destruction.

The most compelling historical analogy for our current moment is the introduction of the automated teller machine, or ATM. When the first ATMs were installed in the 1970s, the logical conclusion was that they would render human bank tellers obsolete. The machine was designed to automate the core tasks of the job: dispensing cash and accepting deposits. The predictions of the era were dire, forecasting the swift demise of the bank teller profession, a stable, middle-class job for hundreds of thousands of people.

The historical data, however, tells a strikingly different story. As the economist James Bessen has documented, despite the rapid and widespread adoption of ATMs across the United

States, the number of human bank tellers did not decline. Instead, between 1980 and 2010, the number of tellers actually grew, from approximately 500,000 to 550,000.[43] This outcome, which directly contradicts the simple logic of automation, is known as the "automation paradox."

The paradox is explained by a series of interconnected economic effects. First, the ATM did indeed reduce the number of tellers required to operate a single bank branch. This is the "displacement effect" in action. But by automating routine transactions, it also dramatically lowered the cost of running a branch. This newfound efficiency made it economically viable for banks to open more physical locations as a key strategy for competing for customer deposits. As a result, the number of urban bank branches in the U.S. surged by more than 40 percent between 1988 and 2004. This expansion in the number of branches created a new demand for tellers that was large enough to more than offset the reduction in tellers per branch.

Most importantly, the technology transformed the nature of the teller's job. With the mundane, transactional elements of their work handled by machines, tellers were freed to focus on higher-value, uniquely human activities. The role evolved from that of a simple cash handler to that of a sales and customer service professional. Tellers became a vital part of the "customer relationship team," responsible for building rapport, solving more complex problems that the machine could not handle, and cross-selling other financial products like credit cards, loans, and investment services. The job was not eliminated; it was redefined and, in many ways, up-skilled.

This historical lesson provides the foundation for a more sophisticated economic understanding of AI's impact, one developed by leading labor economists like Daron Acemoglu and David Autor of the Massachusetts Institute of Technology. Their research argues that the central error in most public debate is the conflation of tasks with jobs.[44] A job is a collection of tasks, and AI, like the ATM, excels at automating specific tasks, particularly those that are routine and rule-based. This creates what economists call a "displacement effect," which puts downward pressure on the demand for labor. However, this is counteracted by a powerful "productivity effect." By making the production of goods and services cheaper, technology increases overall economic activity, which in turn creates a higher demand for labor in the non-automated tasks that remain.

The ultimate balance between these two forces depends on the rate of "new task creation." As technology evolves, it not only automates old tasks but also enables entirely new ones that were previously unimaginable. The internet, for example, automated certain information retrieval tasks but created entirely new professions like web developer, social media manager, and data scientist. The optimistic view holds that AI will be a powerful engine for this kind of new task creation. Acemoglu warns, however, that this is not guaranteed. He expresses concern that too much of the current AI research is focused on what he calls the "Turing Trap": an obsession with creating AI that can perfectly mimic and substitute for human intelligence, rather than creating AI that augments and complements it. A focus on pure substitution leads to a future of displacement, while a focus on augmentation leads to a future of shared prosperity.

This optimistic view of augmentation and new job creation is supported by several major economic forecasts. A 2023 report from Goldman Sachs, while acknowledging that AI could automate tasks equivalent to 300 million full-time jobs, also predicted that the technology could increase annual global GDP by a staggering 7 percent over a decade, creating enormous new wealth and demand.[45] The World Economic Forum's "Future of Jobs Report" projected that while AI and other trends would displace 85 million jobs by 2025, they would also create 97 million new roles, resulting in a net gain of 12 million jobs.[46] These new roles will be in fields like data analysis, AI and machine learning specialization, and process automation: jobs that barely existed a decade ago.

This perspective is championed by leaders like Nvidia's CEO, Jensen Huang, whose company designs the chips that power the AI revolution. He argues that AI will not lead to mass unemployment but will instead create new industries and make existing ones more productive. The real threat, in his view, is not the technology itself, but the failure to adapt to it. His advice to workers is a modern mantra for career resilience: "You're not going to lose your job to an AI, but to someone who knows how to use AI."[47] This sentiment is echoed in a widely cited article from the Harvard Business Review, which states, "AI won't replace humans; but humans with AI will replace humans without AI."[48] This is the core of the optimistic argument: AI is not an autonomous force of destruction, but a powerful tool that will reward those who learn to wield it.

Section 3: Why the Experts Disagree (And Why It Matters)

How can the predictions from intelligent, well-informed experts be so radically different? The chasm between the forecast wall, with its vision of mass unemployment, and the optimistic view of an augmented, prosperous future is not the result of a simple error in calculation. It is the product of fundamentally different assumptions, perspectives, and analytical frameworks. Understanding these points of divergence is not just an academic exercise, it is the key to developing your own clear-eyed strategy. It reveals that the future of work is not a single, predetermined path, but a range of possibilities whose outcome will be shaped by the very factors that cause the experts to disagree.

First, the experts are often operating on different time horizons. The dire warnings from leaders like Dario Amodei and Robert Smith are focused on the immediate, short-term disruption, looking out over the next one to five years. This is the timeframe of corporate budget cycles and immediate competitive pressures. In this window, the displacement effect of automation is likely to be the most visible and painful force, as companies adopt the technology to eliminate existing roles and achieve quick, measurable cost savings. The pain of these layoffs is immediate and concrete, making for powerful headlines and fueling widespread anxiety.

The more optimistic forecasts from institutions like Goldman Sachs and the World Economic Forum, however, tend to look out over a longer, ten-year horizon. This longer view allows for the slower, more complex economic forces to take hold. It provides time for the productivity effect to ripple through the economy, lowering costs, increasing demand, and creating the economic space for new businesses to emerge. It also allows for the creation of new tasks and new jobs to fully materialize, a process that is never instantaneous. The job of a "social media manager" or an "app developer" was not created the day after the internet was commercialized; it took years for the ecosystem to mature to a point where those roles were needed. The experts are not necessarily contradicting each other; they may simply be describing different points on the same long-term curve. The short term may be a period of painful adjustment and significant job loss, while the long term may be one of net growth and reconfigured work. For the individual professional, however, navigating that short-term pain to reach the long-term gain is the central challenge.

Second, the debate is often clouded by a failure to distinguish between tasks, jobs, and careers. This is perhaps the most common and consequential error in the public discourse about AI. When a leader like Satya Nadella says that AI is writing 30 percent of code, he is talking about the automation of tasks. This does not necessarily mean that 30 percent of developer jobs will be eliminated. It is far more likely that the nature of the developer's job will change. Instead of spending their time on the drudgery of writing boilerplate, repetitive code, they can offload that task to an AI assistant. This frees them to focus more of their time and cognitive energy on higher-level challenges: system architecture, creative problem-solving, collaborating with product managers to define user needs, and mentoring junior developers. In this scenario, the job is not destroyed; it is transformed and arguably made more interesting and valuable.

In contrast, a prediction like Jim Farley's, which speaks of replacing half of all white-collar workers, is talking about the elimination of entire jobs. To make this distinction concrete, consider the role of a paralegal. A paralegal's job is a collection of tasks: conducting legal research, reviewing and summarizing vast quantities of documents, drafting initial versions of legal memos, and scheduling depositions. Generative AI is already becoming incredibly proficient at the first three of these tasks. The pessimistic view, which often conflates tasks and jobs, would conclude that since AI can do 75 percent of the work, a law firm can fire 75 percent of its paralegals.

The optimistic, task-based view sees a different future. In this version, the AI handles the laborious and time-consuming drudgery of document review and initial research. The human paralegal, now augmented by this powerful tool, is freed to take on higher-level responsibilities. They can manage more complex cases, spend more time on client communication (a deeply human skill), and develop expertise in managing and verifying the output of the legal AI tools, becoming a new kind of "AI-augmented paralegal." The unit of analysis matters immensely. A focus on tasks leads to a conversation about transformation and upskilling; a focus on jobs leads to a conversation about replacement and obsolescence.

Third, it is impossible to ignore the role of vested interests. The experts making these predictions are not neutral observers; they are participants in the economy with their own incentives and worldviews. The CEO of an AI company, for example, has a clear incentive to highlight the transformative, disruptive power of his technology. This narrative of inevitable, world-changing disruption is a powerful tool for attracting venture capital, recruiting top talent, and creating a sense of urgency for potential customers to adopt their products. A private equity investor may be focused on the short-term cost-cutting potential of AI in the companies he owns, as this directly impacts his returns on investment. Their model is often to acquire a company, increase its efficiency (often through headcount reduction), and sell it for a profit. For them, AI is the ultimate efficiency tool.

Conversely, a global economic body like the World Economic Forum or an academic economist has a different mandate. They are attempting to build a comprehensive model of the entire system, balancing displacement with productivity, considering historical trends, and weighing the broader societal implications. The lens through which an expert views the world inevitably shapes the future they see.

Finally, and perhaps most importantly, many top-down economic forecasts fail to account for the human variable. They often treat the workforce as a passive entity, a collection of roles and skills that will simply be acted upon by technology. This is a form of "techno-determinism": the idea that technology is an autonomous force that moves along a predetermined path, and that society must simply adapt to it. But as the Stanford HAI study on worker preferences demonstrates, this is not how the real world works. Workers are active agents in shaping their own professional lives. They are constantly negotiating their roles, pushing back against the automation of meaningful work, and finding new ways to create value. This human agency is a powerful, unpredictable, and often underestimated force that can significantly alter the trajectory of technological adoption.

Furthermore, the successful adoption of any new technology depends on effective leadership and change management, an area where many organizations are currently failing. A 2025 Gallup poll found that while 44 percent of employees report their organization has begun integrating AI, only 22 percent say their leadership has communicated a clear plan for doing so.[49] This leadership vacuum is a critical wild card. It creates a culture of fear and uncertainty, which itself can hinder the positive adoption of technology. In the absence of a clear strategy, a "shadow AI" culture can emerge, where some employees use AI tools in secret, fearing they will be seen as cheating or incompetent. Others avoid the tools altogether, fearing they will automate themselves out of a job. This failure of leadership prevents companies from realizing the full productivity gains of augmentation and makes the pessimistic forecasts of displacement more likely to become a self-fulfilling prophecy. The future of work is not just an economic equation; it is a deeply human story, and its outcome may depend as much on the quality of our leadership as it does on the quality of our algorithms.

Conclusion

The great debate over AI's impact on the workforce is not a simple academic exercise. It is a high-stakes conversation about our collective future, and as we have seen, the experts are deeply and fundamentally divided. On one side stands the imposing forecast wall, with its stark predictions of mass displacement and a future of technological unemployment, driven by the relentless pursuit of corporate efficiency. On the other stands a more hopeful vision, grounded in historical precedent and economic theory, of a future where humans and machines collaborate to create unprecedented value and new forms of work.

The profound disagreement among experts, rooted in their different time horizons, analytical frameworks, and vested interests, leads to a powerful conclusion for any professional navigating this uncertain landscape: it is impossible to know for sure which forecast will prove to be correct. The future is not yet written. It will be shaped by technological breakthroughs, corporate strategies, government policies, and the choices of millions of individual workers.

Given this deep and unavoidable uncertainty, the only rational strategy is to reject the paralysis of prediction and instead embrace a posture of proactive adaptation. Betting your career on a single forecast: whether optimistic or pessimistic, is a gamble you cannot afford to take. The winning strategy is to build the personal adaptability and resilience to thrive no matter which future unfolds. This means cultivating a skill set that is valuable in a world of widespread displacement and in a world of human-machine augmentation. It means taking control of your own professional development rather than passively waiting to see what happens. The first and most important step in building that adaptability is to look inward and understand the unique, durable, and valuable skills that you possess as a human. It is time to discover your Human Edge.

Chapter 3: The Human Edge: What AI Still Can't Do

Introduction

If a machine can perform your tasks, what is your value? This is not a philosophical question for a distant future; it is the most practical and urgent career question of our time. As we saw in the last chapter, the debate rages on about how many jobs will be lost or changed by artificial intelligence. But beneath the conflicting forecasts lies a more fundamental issue. The AI revolution is not just automating physical labor or simple calculations; it is automating cognitive work. If AI can write code, draft legal briefs, analyze financial statements, and create marketing campaigns, then what is left for us to do? What is the durable, irreplaceable value that a human professional brings to the table when the production of knowledge itself is becoming commoditized?

This chapter provides the definitive answer. It is about moving beyond a defensive crouch and building an offensive strategy. The goal is not to out-compete the machine at its own game of speed and data processing. The goal is to excel at the game a machine cannot play. This requires a deep understanding of your uniquely human advantages. We will introduce a simple yet powerful framework for identifying and cultivating these skills, a model that will serve as your strategic compass for navigating the rest of this book and the rest of your career. It is time to discover your Human Edge.

Section 1: Introducing the C.H.A.T. Model

In an age of intelligent machines, your professional value is no longer defined solely by the technical skills you possess or the tasks you can complete. Your most durable and valuable assets are the capabilities that are intrinsically human. To make these advantages clear and actionable, we can organize them into a memorable framework: the C.H.A.T. Model. This model consists of four pillars that represent the core of the Human Edge:

- Creativity: The ability to imagine, invent, and create something truly new, moving beyond existing patterns.
- Humanity: The capacity for empathy, ethical judgment, mentorship, and building deep, trust-based relationships.
- Adaptability: The skill of learning, unlearning, and navigating ambiguity in a rapidly changing environment.
- Thinking: The application of critical thought, contextual understanding, and common sense to solve complex problems.

This is not just a convenient acronym; it is a framework grounded in the real-world experiences of professionals who are already navigating the AI-integrated workplace. The 2024 Stanford HAI study, "What Workers Really Want from Artificial Intelligence," provides a powerful validation for this model. The study found that while workers are eager for AI to automate the tedious and repetitive parts of their jobs (the drudgery) they instinctively and actively resist its encroachment on tasks that require their core human faculties.[50] The areas they fight to protect, creative strategy, sensitive communication, high-stakes decision-making, and mentoring, map directly onto the four pillars of the C.H.A.T. model.

This resistance is not just fear of change. It is an intuitive recognition of where true professional value lies. Workers know, on a gut level, that their ability to create a novel idea, to connect with a client on an emotional level, to adapt to an unexpected crisis, or to think critically about a flawed plan is what makes them indispensable. They are drawing a line in the sand to protect the very skills that this chapter will teach you to cultivate. The C.H.A.T. model, therefore, is not just a theory; it is a reflection of the strategic ground that human professionals are already defending. It gives a name to the value they know they bring, and it provides a roadmap for strengthening that value in a world where it matters more than ever.

Section 2: A Deep Dive into the Four Pillars

To turn this framework into a practical tool, we need to explore each of the four pillars in detail. By understanding what each one means and why it is so difficult for AI to replicate, you can begin to consciously build your career around these durable strengths.

Creativity: Beyond the Pattern

Modern generative AI is a marvel of pattern recognition and recombination. It can analyze billions of data points, from text and images to musical compositions, and generate new content that is statistically consistent with what it has learned. It can write a sonnet in the style of Shakespeare or create a painting in the style of Van Gogh. But what it cannot do is create a truly original style. It can mimic, but it cannot invent. This is the fundamental distinction between AI-generated content and human creativity.

Human creativity is not just about recombining existing patterns; it is about the imaginative leap that creates a new pattern altogether. It draws on a rich tapestry of lived experience, emotional intuition, cross-disciplinary thinking, and serendipitous discovery. As the futurist Martin Ford notes, jobs that involve "genuinely coming up with new ideas and building something new" are likely to remain "relatively insulated" from AI for the foreseeable future.[51] An AI can be trained on every successful marketing campaign in history, but it cannot generate the truly novel, culture-shifting idea that defines a new era of advertising. It lacks the lived experience and cultural awareness to understand the subtle currents of human desire and aspiration that lead to a breakthrough campaign. It can generate a thousand variations of a car advertisement, but it could not have conceived of Volkswagen's legendary "Think Small" campaign of the 1960s, which broke every rule of car advertising at the time by celebrating a product's smallness and simplicity in an era of excess. That required a deep, contrarian insight into the changing cultural mood, something no algorithm could predict.

Bill Gates, a figure at the center of the technological revolution for decades, has made a similar observation. He predicts that while AI will be a powerful tool for analyzing data in fields like biology and energy, it will not replace the human scientists who formulate the groundbreaking hypotheses that drive true innovation. AI, he argues, "lacks the ability to formulate groundbreaking hypotheses or make intuitive leaps."[52] That intuitive leap, the "aha!" moment that connects two seemingly unrelated ideas, is a hallmark of human creativity. The scientist who realizes that a discovery in marine biology could unlock a problem in materials science is engaging in a form of conceptual blending that is, for now, uniquely human.

The World Economic Forum's "Future of Jobs Report" consistently ranks creative thinking as one of the most important and in-demand skills for the future.[53] This is because in a world where information is abundant and answers are cheap, the ability to ask a new and interesting question becomes more valuable than ever. This shifts the focus from mere problem-solving to the more advanced skill of problem-finding.

An AI is a powerful problem-solver; you can give it a well-defined objective, and it can work tirelessly to find an optimal solution. But it cannot identify a problem that no one has thought to solve yet. It cannot walk through a hospital and see a flaw in the patient check-in process that is causing unnecessary stress, and then imagine a completely new system to fix it. That requires empathy, observation, and the creative spark to see a better way. The professional who can envision a new product, design a novel business model, or craft a compelling and original story will always have an edge over a machine that is, by its very nature, bound by the data of the past.

Humanity: The Power of Connection and Conscience

Artificial intelligence has no emotions, no consciousness, and no conscience. It can be programmed to simulate empathy, but it cannot genuinely feel it. This makes the entire spectrum of skills related to human connection, emotional intelligence, and ethical judgment a durable and powerful advantage.

Consider the professions that are most deeply rooted in human interaction. A therapist relies on building a foundation of trust and rapport, reading the subtle emotional cues in a patient's voice and body language, and offering genuine compassion. A great teacher does more than just deliver information; she inspires curiosity, mentors students through personal challenges, and creates a supportive classroom environment. A successful leader motivates her team not just with data and directives, but with empathy, vision, and the ability to build a cohesive and trusting culture. As one analysis noted, these are qualities that "AI struggles to replicate."[54] An AI can provide information, but it cannot provide wisdom, inspiration, or a shoulder to cry on. These deeply human interactions require a shared vulnerability and a sense of genuine presence that a machine cannot fake.

This human-centric advantage extends beyond the traditionally "caring" professions. In business, ethical judgment is becoming an increasingly valuable skill. AI systems are powerful tools, but they are also prone to inheriting the biases present in their training data, and they are incapable of making nuanced moral decisions. This creates a critical need for human oversight. A pricing algorithm, for example, might be ruthlessly efficient at maximizing profit, but it lacks the ethical framework to consider issues of fairness or brand reputation.

A compelling case study comes from the global retailer H&M, which developed a sophisticated AI to manage markdowns for its end-of-season inventory. The company quickly realized that a purely algorithmic approach could lead to brand-damaging decisions, such as pricing items in a way that seemed unfair to customers or creating a perception of cheapness that undermined the brand's long-term value. Instead of full automation, H&M implemented a "human-in-the-loop" system. The AI provides data-driven pricing recommendations, but human merchandisers are integrated into the workflow to review, adjust, and approve the final prices. They bring their contextual knowledge of the market (e.g., knowing that a local festival might impact sales of a certain item), their understanding of the brand's values, and their ethical judgment to the process. This collaborative approach, combining the AI's analytical power with human oversight, led to demonstrably better business results than either the AI or the human experts could achieve on their own.[55]

This shift is being recognized at the highest levels of corporate strategy. Amala Duggirala, a senior executive at the financial services organization USAA, described her company's evolving hiring philosophy in response to AI. "The employee value proposition [is] shifting to skills that are uniquely human, and moving away from skills that machines can master," she explained. "Our planning and intent are oriented toward giving employees the opportunities and training to adapt as the work environment changes."[56] In an age of automation, your humanity is not a soft skill; it is a hard asset. It is the foundation of trust, the source of ethical stewardship, and the engine of effective collaboration and leadership.

Adaptability: The Ultimate Power Skill

If there is one skill that stands above all others in an era of rapid and unpredictable change, it is adaptability. The ability to learn, unlearn, and relearn in response to new technologies and shifting market demands is the ultimate career insurance. Technical skills will always have a shelf life, but the capacity to adapt is timeless.

The data on this is overwhelming. LinkedIn's analysis of the most in-demand skills consistently places adaptability near the top of the list.[57] The World Economic Forum's research identifies a cluster of self-management skills, including "resilience, flexibility and agility", as being among the top three capabilities that companies say they need most.[58] The reason is simple: in a world where, according to PwC, the required skills for AI-exposed jobs are changing 66 percent faster than for other jobs, the ability to keep pace is no longer optional.[59]

Nvidia's CEO, Jensen Huang, whose company's technology is powering much of the AI revolution, has argued that in this new environment, "the most valuable skill may not be technical ability, but adaptability."[60] He urges workers at all levels to be ready to "embrace AI" and continuously adjust, rather than clinging to old methods. This is not just about learning to use a new piece of software. It is about cultivating a mindset of continuous growth and intellectual curiosity. It is about being willing to step outside your comfort zone, experiment with new tools, and see failure not as a setback, but as a learning opportunity.

This concept is closely related to the work of Stanford psychologist Carol Dweck on "growth mindset" versus "fixed mindset." An individual with a fixed mindset believes their abilities are static and unchangeable. When faced with a challenge like AI, their primary reaction is fear and resistance, as the new technology threatens their established sense of competence. In contrast, an individual with a growth mindset believes their abilities can be developed through dedication and hard work. They see a challenge like AI not as a threat, but as an opportunity to learn and grow.

Consider two employees in a marketing department where a new AI-powered analytics tool is introduced. The employee with a fixed mindset avoids the tool, complains that it is too complicated, and worries that it will make their job irrelevant. The employee with a growth mindset, however, dives in. They take the online tutorials, experiment with the tool on a small project, and actively look for ways it can make their work better. Within a few months, the second employee has become the team's go-to expert on the new system, while the first employee has fallen behind. This is adaptability in action.

As one LinkedIn executive put it, "Adaptability is the best way to have agency right now. At the core of managing change is building that muscle of adaptability."[61] In a world of constant disruption, the flexible will inherit the earth.

Thinking: The Application of Judgment

The final pillar of the Human Edge is thinking: specifically, the application of critical thought, contextual understanding, and common sense. While it may seem counterintuitive, in an age where AI can provide instant answers, the ability to think clearly and critically has become more valuable, not less.

Modern large language models are masters of generating plausible-sounding text, but they have a well-known and dangerous flaw: they "hallucinate." Because they operate on statistical patterns rather than a true understanding of the world, they can generate information that is factually incorrect, nonsensical, or subtly biased, all while delivering it with an air of complete authority. They have no concept of truth or falsehood. This makes the human in the loop, the critical thinker who can vet the AI's output, more important than ever. The professional who blindly trusts an AI's answer is a liability; the professional who can critically evaluate it, cross-reference it, and identify its flaws is indispensable. Imagine a junior lawyer asking an AI to find precedents for a legal case. The AI, in a hallucination, could invent a plausible but entirely fictional case law, which, if not caught by the human lawyer, could lead to a disastrous legal strategy.

Furthermore, AI lacks common sense and a grounded understanding of the physical and social world. It has never unclogged a toilet, navigated a difficult office political situation, or felt the disappointment of a failed project. Its knowledge is derived entirely from the text and data it was trained on, leaving it with significant blind spots. This is why humans will always be needed to handle novel situations, to solve problems that do not fit a pre-existing pattern, and to apply judgment in ambiguous, high-stakes environments. An AI can analyze sales data, but it cannot understand the subtle context that a seasoned sales manager knows: that a key competitor just launched a new product, that a major client is undergoing a leadership change, or that a recent news event has made customers anxious. This contextual awareness is a form of thinking that is deeply human.

The ability to ask the right questions is another facet of critical thinking that is becoming a premium skill. An AI is a powerful answer engine, but it is only as good as the questions it is asked. The skill of prompt engineering, crafting precise and insightful queries to elicit the best possible response from an AI, is an emerging discipline. But beyond the technical skill of writing a good prompt lies the strategic skill of knowing what to ask in the first place. The professional who can correctly diagnose a business problem, formulate a key strategic question, and then use AI as a tool to explore potential answers is operating at a much higher level than someone who is simply asking for factual recall.

Conclusion

The rise of the intelligent machine does not devalue human capability; it clarifies it. It forces us to distinguish between the tasks that can be automated and the skills that are uniquely human. The *C.H.A.T. model* provides a clear and actionable framework for understanding these durable skills. *Creativity* allows us to innovate beyond the patterns of the past. *Humanity* enables us to connect, empathize, and make ethical judgments. *Adaptability* gives us the resilience to thrive amid constant change. And *Thinking* allows us to apply critical judgment to a world overflowing with information.

These four pillars are not just abstract concepts; they are the foundation of an offensive career strategy. They are not separate and distinct, but work together in a dynamic way. Your critical thinking guides how you adapt to new tools. Your humanity informs the problems your creativity sets out to solve. By consciously assessing your own strengths across these domains and proactively seeking opportunities to develop them, you can align your career with the work that is most meaningful, most fulfilling, and most resilient to automation. The goal is to make yourself so uniquely human that no machine can ever be a true substitute.

Now that you have a clear understanding of what your Human Edge is, the next part of this book will provide a tactical playbook for how to build it. We will turn from theory to practice, starting with the specific strategies that early-career professionals can use to launch a career that is future-proof from day one.

PART II: START SMART: FOR EARLY-CAREER PROFESSIONALS

Chapter 4: Where AI Can't Go (Yet)

Introduction

"Until a mobile robot can unclog a toilet or hang drywall, trade jobs are pretty safe from AI."[62] This blunt assessment, from a report on the future of skilled trades, cuts through the abstract anxieties about artificial intelligence and grounds the conversation in a simple, physical reality. While an AI can write a poem, analyze a stock portfolio, or even pass the bar exam, it cannot yet navigate the messy, unpredictable, and often physically demanding environments of the real world. Its intelligence is vast but disembodied.

This reveals a fascinating contradiction at the heart of artificial intelligence, a phenomenon known as Moravec's paradox. In the 1980s, robotics researchers like Hans Moravec observed that, contrary to traditional assumptions, the things that are hardest for humans (like advanced mathematics, formal logic, and games like chess) are relatively easy for computers. Conversely, the things that are easiest for humans, like recognizing a face, picking up a cup, or walking across a room, are incredibly difficult for machines. A four-year-old child possesses a level of sensory perception and physical dexterity that is far beyond the capabilities of the most advanced robot. This is because these skills, honed over millions of years of evolution, are deeply encoded in our biology. AI's intelligence, for now, exists in the digital realm of data and algorithms. It lacks a body, and this fundamental limitation creates entire zones of the economy where the demand for human skill, dexterity, and presence remains robust

For early-career professionals charting a course, understanding these limitations is not just an academic exercise; it is a strategic necessity. It allows you to move beyond a defensive posture of worrying which jobs will disappear and adopt an offensive strategy of targeting the career paths where AI's current weaknesses are your greatest strengths. This chapter is a map to those safe zones. We will explore the three primary categories of resilient careers: those that are deeply human-centered and hands-on, those that fuse AI literacy with human expertise, and the entirely new jobs being created by the AI revolution itself.

Section 1: Human-Centered and Hands-On Roles

The first and most durable category of AI-resistant careers includes roles that require a high degree of physical dexterity, complex real-world interaction, and genuine human empathy. These are jobs that cannot be performed from behind a screen or reduced to a set of predictable, data-driven tasks. They are grounded in the physical and emotional realities of human experience, the very domains where Moravec's paradox is most apparent.

The most obvious examples are the skilled trades. The work of an electrician, a plumber, a carpenter, or an HVAC technician involves navigating unique and unstructured environments every single day. No two leaky pipes or faulty wiring systems are exactly alike. These jobs require a sophisticated blend of skills that AI cannot replicate. This includes sensory perception: the ability to feel the subtle tension in a wire, to hear the specific hum of a malfunctioning motor, or to smell the faint scent of burning insulation. It requires advanced spatial reasoning to visualize how pipes and wires run through the hidden spaces of a building. And it demands constant improvisation and physical problem-solving to adapt to unforeseen complications on a job site. This is why a recent survey found that 65 percent of tradespeople feel their jobs are secure from AI-driven automation.[63] A robot may be able to perform a repetitive task on an assembly line with superhuman precision, but it lacks the general-purpose mobility and problem-solving capabilities to diagnose and repair a complex issue inside the wall of a century-old house.

Beyond the physical, roles centered on human care and connection possess a deep and lasting resilience. The healthcare industry provides a powerful example. While AI is becoming a formidable tool for diagnostics, analyzing medical images and identifying patterns in patient data with incredible accuracy, it cannot replace the human element of caregiving. Consider the role of a nurse practitioner, a profession projected to grow by an astonishing 45 percent between 2022 and 2032.[64] A nurse's value extends far beyond administering medication or taking vital signs. It involves comforting a frightened patient, explaining a complex treatment plan to a concerned family, and using intuition honed by years of experience to notice subtle changes in a patient's condition. These are acts of empathy and holistic judgment that are, for the foreseeable future, exclusively human. The trust a patient places in a caregiver is built on a foundation of shared humanity, eye contact, and the sense of being truly seen and heard.

Similarly, the demand for mental health counselors is expected to surge by 20 to 22 percent, driven by a growing societal recognition of the importance of mental well-being.[65] An

AI chatbot might be able to offer scripted advice based on cognitive-behavioral therapy principles, but it cannot form the therapeutic alliance, the bond of trust and genuine human connection, that is the foundation of effective counseling. The work of a therapist involves navigating the complex, often contradictory landscape of human emotion, a task that requires a level of emotional intelligence far beyond any algorithm. The same holds true for physical therapists, who combine medical knowledge with hands-on skill to help patients recover from injury. They must physically guide a patient's movements, provide encouragement through painful rehabilitation, and build a trusting relationship that motivates the patient to stick with their recovery plan.

The field of education follows the same pattern. An AI can be an excellent tutor, providing personalized instruction and endless practice problems, as we see with tools like Khanmigo. However, it cannot replace the role of a K-12 teacher. A teacher's job is not just to transmit information, but to manage a classroom of diverse personalities, to inspire a love of learning, to mentor students through the social and emotional challenges of growing up, and to create a safe and engaging learning environment. This is a real-time, multi-agent social challenge that requires a dynamic awareness and emotional intelligence that are far beyond the capabilities of any current AI system. A teacher can spot the student who is having a bad day from a subtle shift in their posture, mediate a conflict between friends during recess, and adapt a lesson plan on the fly when they see the class is not engaged.

These human-centered and hands-on professions are not "anti-technology." A modern mechanic uses sophisticated diagnostic computers, and a surgeon may use a robot for enhanced precision. But in all these roles, technology is a tool in the hands of a human expert, not a replacement for them. The core value is delivered through human skill, judgment, and presence. For those seeking a career with a low risk of automation, these fields offer a powerful and stable foundation.

Section 2: The Rise of Hybrid "AI + X" Roles

The second category of resilient careers does not involve running away from AI, but running toward it. These are the hybrid or "fusion" roles that sit at the intersection of technological literacy and deep domain expertise. Professionals in these roles are not just users of AI; they are the critical bridge between the technology's capabilities and real-world business needs. They are the "AI translators" who can speak both the language of the machine and the language of their industry, creating value that neither side could create alone.

This is the "AI + X" model, where X represents a traditional field of expertise. Think of it as a formula for creating a high-value, future-proof career: AI + Law, AI + Medicine, AI + Finance, or AI + Urban Planning. The professional who embodies this fusion is not easily replaced, because they possess a combination of skills that is rare and powerful. They act as a human API (Application Programming Interface), connecting the raw power of the AI to the specific, nuanced problems of their field.

Consider the emerging role of an AI Ethics Consultant. As companies deploy AI systems that make decisions affecting people's lives, from loan applications and hiring selections to medical diagnoses, they face a complex web of ethical and regulatory risks. An AI model cannot audit itself for bias or ensure its decisions are fair and transparent. This requires a human expert who understands both the technical workings of machine learning and the nuances of ethical philosophy, corporate responsibility, and anti-discrimination law. This is a classic AI + X role, combining AI literacy with expertise in ethics and law.

Similarly, the role of an AI Product Manager is becoming increasingly vital. A team of brilliant data scientists might be able to build a powerful new AI model, but they may not have the business acumen to identify the most valuable customer problem it can solve or the user experience skills to design a product that is intuitive and easy to use. The AI Product Manager fills this gap. They are responsible for defining the product vision, translating customer needs into technical requirements, and guiding the development process to ensure the final product is not just technologically impressive, but also commercially successful and genuinely useful. This role requires a blend of AI knowledge, business strategy, and user-centered design thinking. A 2025 analysis from LinkedIn highlighted this trend, noting that professionals who can combine AI skills with strategic design thinking are commanding significant salary premiums, as companies are desperate for leaders who can build AI-powered products that people actually want to use.[66]

The AI + X model can be applied to virtually any field, creating a new class of augmented professionals. An AI + Journalist will use AI tools to analyze massive datasets to uncover stories of public interest, but will apply their human skills of storytelling, source verification, and ethical judgment to report on them. An AI + Financial Advisor will use AI to run complex retirement simulations for their clients, but will use their human empathy and communication skills to understand a client's life goals and risk tolerance, providing personalized advice that goes beyond the numbers. An AI + UX Designer will use generative AI to create dozens of initial design mockups, but will use their deep understanding of human psychology and usability principles to select and refine the design that will provide the most intuitive and enjoyable user experience. An AI + Architect can use generative tools to explore thousands of sustainable building designs that meet specific energy efficiency constraints, but will apply their human aesthetic judgment and understanding of community needs to select the final design.

These fusion roles are inherently defensible because they require a combination of left-brain and right-brain skills. They demand that you be both technically literate and humanistically wise. The value is not in the AI skill alone, nor in the domain expertise alone, but in the synthesis of the two. For early-career professionals, this presents a clear strategic path: do not just learn about AI in a vacuum. Learn about AI in the context of a field you are passionate about. Become the person who can bridge the gap, and you will make yourself indispensable.

Section 3: New Jobs Created by AI

The final category of resilient careers consists of the entirely new job titles that are being born from the AI revolution itself. History shows that major technological shifts are always a force of what the economist Joseph Schumpeter called "creative destruction." While some old jobs are eliminated, new and often previously unimaginable jobs are created. The rise of the automobile displaced the blacksmith and the carriage maker, but it created the auto mechanic, the assembly line worker, the highway engineer, and the entire suburban real estate industry. The internet automated the work of the travel agent and the encyclopedia salesman, but it created the web developer, the social media manager, and the search engine optimization specialist.

AI is proving to be no different. The World Economic Forum, in its comprehensive "Future of Jobs Report," projects that AI will be a net job creator, leading to the emergence of 97 million new roles by 2025.[67] While it is impossible to predict all of these new titles, we can already see the clear outlines of several emerging professions that are rapidly moving from the fringe to the mainstream.

One of the most prominent new roles is the Prompt Engineer. This job did not exist a few years ago, and now major companies are hiring for these positions with six-figure salaries. A prompt engineer is, in essence, a skilled communicator who specializes in talking to AI models. This is far more complex than simply asking a question. It involves understanding the architecture and nuances of large language models and crafting highly specific and sophisticated prompts to elicit the most accurate, relevant, and creative responses. A skilled prompt engineer knows how to provide context, set constraints, define a persona for the AI, and iterate on a prompt to refine the output. It is a role that is part creative writer, part computer programmer, and part psychologist. As AI models become more powerful and integrated into business workflows, the ability to effectively query them becomes a high-value skill.

Another critical new role is the AI Auditor. As we have discussed, AI systems can be black boxes, and they are prone to errors, biases, and hallucinations. An AI Auditor is a professional who is tasked with independently testing and validating the outputs of these systems to ensure they are fair, accurate, and compliant with regulations. This might involve designing tests to probe an AI hiring tool for gender or racial bias, or auditing a financial AI to ensure its lending decisions are explainable and non-discriminatory. With new regulations like the EU AI Act coming into force, this is quickly moving from a "nice-to-have" ethical consideration to a legally mandated compliance function. This role requires a unique combination of technical understanding, statistical knowledge, and a strong ethical compass.

The creative industries are also seeing the birth of new roles. The title of Generative Art Director is beginning to appear. This is not just a graphic designer who uses AI tools. It is a creative leader who curates and directs the output of multiple generative models, blending and refining AI-generated elements with human artistry to create a final, cohesive visual campaign. They are the conductors of a new kind of digital orchestra, using their artistic vision to guide the powerful but unthinking creativity of the machine. They might use one AI to generate a background, another to create a character, and then use their own skills in a tool like Photoshop to composite the elements and add the final human touch.

Other new roles on the horizon include AI Trainers, who are responsible for fine-tuning and customizing general AI models for specific business tasks. This involves curating high-quality datasets and using techniques like Reinforcement Learning from Human Feedback (RLHF) to teach the AI the specific nuances of a company's brand voice or customer service philosophy. We are also seeing the rise of the AI Business Strategist, a senior role that goes beyond product management to advise companies on how to fundamentally redesign their business models to take advantage of the new capabilities that AI unlocks. These new professions demonstrate that AI is not just a job destroyer; it is a job creator. For the early-career professional with a sense of curiosity and a willingness to learn, these emerging fields represent a ground-floor opportunity to build a career in a high-growth, high-demand area.

Conclusion

The landscape of work is being reshaped by artificial intelligence, but this does not mean that the future is a barren wasteland of unemployment. On the contrary, it is a landscape rich with opportunity for those who know where to look. As we have seen, there are at least three major categories of resilient career paths. The human-centered and hands-on roles leverage our physical dexterity and our capacity for empathy in ways that disembodied AI cannot. The hybrid "AI + X" roles create immense value by fusing technological literacy with deep domain expertise. And the entirely new jobs created by AI offer a chance to become a pioneer in an emerging field.

What all these paths have in common is that they lean into uniquely human strengths. They are built on the pillars of the C.H.A.T. model: Creativity, Humanity, Adaptability, and Thinking. This is not just a hopeful theory; it is a trend supported by hard economic data. The same Stanford HAI study that identified workers' desire to protect their meaningful work also forecasts that the economic value of interpersonal skills is set to rise significantly in the coming years.[68] As routine cognitive tasks are automated, the skills that will command a premium are precisely those that machines lack: communication, collaboration, mentorship, and leadership. By choosing a career path that is grounded in these human-centric skills, you are not just hedging against automation; you are aligning your career with the future of value creation. You are choosing to armor up with the skills that matter most.

Now that you know where the safe zones are, the next chapter will provide a tactical guide for how to get there. We will explore how to hack the new AI-driven hiring systems to land a job in one of these resilient fields.

Chapter 5: Hack the Hiring System

Introduction

Before you can impress a hiring manager, you have to get past the gatekeeper. For decades, that gatekeeper was a human being in the human resources department, a person who would manually sift through a stack of paper resumes, relying on experience and intuition. Today, that gatekeeper is an algorithm. An estimated 99 percent of Fortune 500 companies, along with a vast and growing number of smaller businesses, now use an Applicant Tracking System (ATS) to manage the hiring process.[69] This software is the first, and often most formidable, hurdle in any modern job search. It is the first AI you must impress.

Companies have adopted these systems for compelling reasons. Faced with a deluge of online applications, the ATS provides a way to manage the sheer volume, ensure a degree of consistency, and maintain compliance with hiring regulations. For a recruiter, it is an indispensable tool for bringing order to chaos. But for a job applicant, it is an impersonal, unforgiving sentinel. The ATS scans, parses, and ranks your application, deciding in a fraction of a second whether it is worthy of human eyes. It does not appreciate your unique career journey or the subtle nuances of your experience. It simply looks for patterns and keywords. If your resume is not optimized for the machine, it will likely be discarded into a digital void, no matter how qualified you are.

This is the new reality of the corporate world. Landing a job is no longer a purely human-to-human interaction. It is a two-stage challenge that requires a two-audience strategy. First, you must write for the machine to pass the filter. This is a technical, analytical process of optimization. Then, and only then, do you get the chance to write for the human, where you must capture their attention, tell a compelling story, and prove your value. This chapter is your guide to hacking this new system. We will deconstruct the AI gatekeeper and provide a tactical playbook for crafting an application that satisfies the algorithm while captivating the person on the other side.

Section 1: Writing for the Machine: Passing the AI Filter

The primary function of an Applicant Tracking System is to make a recruiter's life manageable. Faced with hundreds of applications for a single opening, they use the ATS to automate the initial screening process. The software works by parsing your resume, breaking down the text to extract key pieces of information like your contact details, work history, education, and skills, and storing it in a searchable database. When a recruiter needs to find candidates, they do not read every resume. They search the database using keywords and filters related to the job description. The ATS then ranks applicants based on how well their resumes match those keywords. Your first goal, therefore, is to ensure your resume is both machine-readable and keyword-rich.

Creating a machine-readable, or AI-friendly, resume is a technical exercise in simplicity and clarity. The parsing algorithms used by these systems are powerful, but they are also surprisingly brittle. They are programmed to look for information in expected places and can be easily confused by complex or unconventional formatting. This means that the beautifully designed, multi-column resume you created in a program like Canva or Adobe Illustrator might look impressive to a human, but it could be completely indecipherable to an ATS. The software may fail to correctly identify the different sections, jumbling your work experience with your education or failing to extract your skills altogether.

To avoid this digital rejection, you must adhere to a few fundamental best practices for resume formatting. Think of it as building a clean, well-structured webpage for a search engine to crawl.

First, use a clean, single-column layout with a standard, reverse-chronological format (your most recent job first). Avoid tables, text boxes, and columns, as these elements can disrupt the parser's ability to read the document linearly from top to bottom. Use standard, web-safe fonts like Georgia, Arial, or Calibri; exotic or custom fonts may not render correctly. It is also wise to avoid placing important information, like your name or contact details, in the header or footer of the document, as some older ATS parsers are programmed to ignore these sections.

Second, use conventional headings for your sections. This is not the place for creative flair. Instead of titles like "Where I've Been" or "What I Can Do," stick to the unambiguous standards that the ATS is programmed to recognize: "Work Experience," "Professional Experience," "Education," and "Skills." This ensures the software correctly categorizes your information, making it searchable for the recruiter. Use standard bullet points, the simple round or square ones, rather than fancy symbols or icons.

Finally, pay attention to the file type. While PDF is often preferred for preserving formatting for the human reader, a

.docx file can sometimes be a safer bet for the ATS. Some older systems struggle to parse PDFs correctly, especially if they contain complex elements. If the application portal gives you a choice, a .docx file is often the most compatible option for the machine.

Once your resume is machine-readable, the next step is to make it keyword-rich. This is the heart of the optimization process. The ATS does not understand nuance; it understands keyword matching. Your task is to strategically mirror the language of the job description in your resume. Begin by carefully deconstructing the job posting. Copy and paste the text into a document and highlight the key skills, qualifications, and responsibilities. Look for both hard skills (specific software, programming languages, or technical abilities like "Python," "Salesforce," or "financial modeling") and soft skills (transferable qualities like "project management," "team leadership," or "strategic communication").

Create a master list of these keywords and then systematically weave them into your resume. A dedicated "Skills" or "Core Competencies" section near the top of your resume is an excellent place to list many of these keywords, providing a quick, scannable summary for both the AI and the human reader. But do not stop there. The most effective way to integrate keywords is to use them in the bullet points describing your work experience. This provides context and demonstrates how you have applied those skills.

For example, if a job description for a marketing role repeatedly mentions "SEO strategy," "content marketing," and "Google Analytics," you must ensure those exact phrases appear in your resume. Do not assume the AI will understand that "search engine work" is the same as "SEO strategy." You must use the precise terminology. This does not mean you should engage in "keyword stuffing," the practice of cramming as many keywords as possible into your resume in an unnatural way. A human will eventually read your resume, and it needs to be coherent and compelling. The goal is to describe your accomplishments using the language that the company itself uses. For instance, instead of writing a generic bullet point like "Managed social media," you could write an optimized one like "Developed and executed a comprehensive content marketing strategy across multiple platforms, resulting in a 25% increase in engagement and leveraging Google Analytics to refine our SEO strategy." This phrasing is not only rich with keywords but also demonstrates tangible results, making it appealing to both the machine and the human reader.

Modern tools like LinkedIn Recruiter 2024 have made this keyword-driven approach even more central to the hiring process. Recruiters on these platforms use sophisticated filters to search for candidates, combining keywords with criteria like years of experience, industry, and location. By optimizing your resume and your LinkedIn profile with the right keywords, you are not just trying to pass a filter for a single job application; you are making yourself discoverable to a vast network of recruiters who are constantly searching for talent.

Section 2: Standing Out to the Human: The "Proof of Work" Imperative

Passing the AI filter is a necessary but insufficient step. It gets your resume into the "maybe" pile, but it does not get you the interview. The second, and more challenging, part of the process is to stand out to the human recruiter who is now facing a deluge of perfectly optimized, AI-generated applications. This is the new "AI arms race" in hiring. As more candidates use AI tools to write and optimize their resumes, recruiters are being flooded with applications that all look remarkably similar. One recent report found that a single corporate job opening can attract an average of 588 applications.[70] No human can meaningfully review that many documents. They will spend, at most, a few seconds glancing at each resume that the ATS serves up.

In this environment, a generic, keyword-optimized resume is no longer enough. It might be technically perfect, but it lacks a soul. It does not tell a story, convey a personality, or provide compelling evidence of your abilities. This is where the concept of "proof of work" becomes your most powerful differentiator. It is the tangible evidence that you can do what you say you can do. This can take many forms: a portfolio of your design work, a link to a live web application you built, a blog post where you share your insights on an industry trend, or a detailed case study of a project you led.

The demand for this kind of tangible proof is a direct response to the flood of generic applications. Hiring managers are becoming increasingly skeptical of resumes alone. They want to see the work. As one hiring newsletter bluntly put it, modern recruiters are now prioritizing projects over GPAs. A recruiter quoted in a recent industry report captured this sentiment perfectly: "I ask for the GitHub or the results."[71] They want to see your code, your designs, your writing, your analysis. This is because a portfolio provides a much richer signal of your capabilities than a list of bullet points on a resume. It demonstrates your skills, your curiosity, your problem-solving process, and your ability to create real-world value.

This shift toward proof of work aligns perfectly with the findings of the Stanford HAI study, which predicted that the economic value of interpersonal and human-centric skills would rise as routine tasks become automated.[72] Your portfolio is the ultimate showcase for these skills. A well-documented project does not just display your technical abilities; it demonstrates your Creativity in coming up with the idea, your Humanity in understanding the needs of the user, your Adaptability in learning the tools to build it, and your critical Thinking in executing the strategy. It brings the C.H.A.T. model to life.

To make this concrete, imagine a recruiter looking at two candidates for a junior data analyst role. The first candidate has a perfectly optimized resume. It hits all the right keywords (e.g., "Python," "SQL," "Tableau," "data visualization") and the work experience is described with strong action verbs. It is a good resume that will pass the ATS screen. The second candidate's resume is also well-optimized, but it includes a link to a personal website. On that website, the recruiter finds a blog post titled, "How I Used Public Transit Data to Find the Best Place for a New Coffee Shop in My City." The post includes a detailed explanation of the project, snippets of the Python code used for the analysis, and several compelling data visualizations created in Tableau that clearly tell a story.

Which candidate do you think gets the interview? The second one, almost every time. The first candidate claims to have the skills. The second candidate has proven it. The blog post is a powerful piece of proof of work that demonstrates not only technical competence but also curiosity, initiative, and the ability to apply skills to a real-world problem. This is how you stand out in a sea of sameness.

The cover letter also plays a new and vital role in this context. It is no longer a formal, dry summary of your resume. It is your primary tool for storytelling. It is where you connect the dots for the recruiter, explaining why you are passionate about this specific company and how your proof of work directly relates to the challenges they are facing. It is your chance to inject your human voice into an otherwise sterile process.

Section 3: Beyond the Resume: AI in the Interview Process

The influence of AI in the hiring process does not end with the resume screen. It is increasingly being used in the interview stage itself, creating new challenges and opportunities for candidates. The most common form of this is the asynchronous, or one-way, video interview. A recent survey found that 61 percent of organizations now use this method, particularly for initial screening.[73]

In a one-way video interview, you are not speaking to a live person. Instead, you are presented with a series of pre-recorded questions on your screen and given a short amount of time to record your answers. These recordings are then analyzed by an AI before being passed on to a human recruiter. The AI can be programmed to analyze a wide range of signals. It uses speech-to-text technology to transcribe your answers and then scans the transcript for keywords from the job description. It can analyze your tone of voice, your speaking pace, and your use of filler words like "um" and "ah." Some more advanced systems even claim to analyze facial expressions and eye contact to gauge confidence and engagement, though the scientific validity of this is highly debated.

Performing well in this format requires a different set of skills than a traditional interview. First, preparation is paramount. You must treat it with the same seriousness as a live interview. Set up in a quiet, well-lit space with a professional, uncluttered background. Test your camera and microphone beforehand. Dress as you would for an in-person meeting. Second, because you are speaking to a camera, you must be intentional about conveying energy and engagement. Look directly at the camera lens, not at your own image on the screen, to simulate eye contact. A useful trick is to place a small, friendly sticker, like a smiley face, next to your webcam to give you a focal point. Speak clearly and at a moderate pace, and be mindful of your tone of voice.

Third, structure your answers logically. A useful framework is the STAR method (Situation, Task, Action, Result). This method of storytelling is not only compelling to human listeners but also easy for an AI to parse, as it provides a clear, structured narrative. When you are asked a behavioral question, such as "Tell me about a time you faced a difficult challenge," begin by describing the Situation, explain the Task you needed to accomplish, detail the Action you took, and conclude with the positive Result of your actions. This provides a complete and satisfying answer that demonstrates your problem-solving abilities.

Beyond one-way interviews, some companies are also using AI-powered skills assessments and games to evaluate candidates. These can range from online coding challenges for technical roles to gamified assessments from platforms like Pymetrics that measure cognitive and emotional traits like focus, risk tolerance, and altruism. The key to success in these assessments is practice. Many platforms offer sample tests, and familiarizing yourself with the format can significantly reduce anxiety and improve your performance.

While the prospect of being interviewed by an AI can be intimidating, it also offers an advantage. You can turn the technology into your own personal interview coach. Use a tool like ChatGPT to generate common interview questions for your target role. Then, record yourself answering them on video. Watch the playback and critique your own performance. Are you making eye contact? Is your energy level high? Are your answers clear and concise? You can even use AI tools to transcribe your answers and check them for clarity and the use of relevant keywords. By using AI as your practice partner, you can build the confidence and polish needed to excel when the real recording begins.

Conclusion

The modern hiring landscape is a complex, multi-stage process governed by a new set of rules. The rise of AI has created a system where you must appeal to two very different audiences: the machine and the human. Hacking this system requires a deliberate, two-pronged strategy. The first part of your strategy is technical. You must create a clean, machine-readable resume and optimize it with the precise keywords that the Applicant Tracking System is looking for. This is the price of admission, the step that gets you past the initial gatekeeper. It is a game of technical compliance, and you must play it to win.

The second part of your strategy is deeply human. Once you have passed the AI filter, you must capture the attention of an overwhelmed human recruiter. In a world of AI-generated resumes, you must differentiate yourself with a compelling narrative and tangible proof of work. Your portfolio, your projects, and your ability to tell a story about your skills are what will make you memorable. This is where you showcase your creativity, your critical thinking, and your passion: the qualities that no machine can replicate. This two-audience approach extends to the interview process, where you must be prepared to demonstrate your capabilities to both an algorithm and a person.

By mastering this dual strategy, you can turn a daunting and opaque process into a manageable one. You can learn to speak the language of the machine without losing your human voice. Now that you know how to get past the gatekeepers and land the job, the next chapter will show you how to use AI as your own personal tool for success, helping you learn faster and work smarter from day one.

Chapter 6: Work With AI, From Day One

Introduction

A user on the social media platform Reddit recently shared a story that perfectly captures the new reality of preparing for a professional career. He had a big job interview coming up and was feeling nervous and unprepared. Instead of just reading articles or practicing in front of a mirror, he opened ChatGPT. He fed the AI the job description and his resume, and then asked it to act as the hiring manager and conduct a mock interview. The AI generated a series of tough, relevant questions. He answered them out loud, and then asked the AI for feedback. It analyzed his responses, pointed out areas where he could be more specific, and suggested ways to better align his experience with the company's needs. He repeated this process for hours, running through different scenarios and refining his answers until, as he put it, he felt "completely ready." He aced the real interview and got the job.[74]

This is not a story about cheating. It is a story about smart leveraging. The user did not ask the AI to take the interview for him; he used it as a tireless, on-demand coach to make himself better. This represents a profound psychological shift in how we should approach our careers. It is a move away from viewing AI as a mysterious or threatening force and toward seeing it as a powerful personal tool for empowerment. The question is no longer if you should use AI at work, but how you can use it to accelerate your learning, amplify your productivity, and deliver more value from the very first day of your career. This chapter is your guide to doing just that. We will explore the three-part strategy for immediate impact: how to use AI as your personal tutor, how to make it your productivity engine, and how to navigate the ethical boundaries that come with this powerful new tool.

Section 1: AI as Your Personal Tutor

One of the greatest challenges of starting a new job is the steep learning curve. You are expected to quickly absorb a vast amount of new information: the company's culture, its internal processes, the technical details of its products, and the specific skills required for your role. In the past, this learning process relied heavily on the availability of patient colleagues and supportive managers. Your ability to get up to speed was often limited by how much time others were willing to invest in you. Today, you have access to a new kind of mentor, one that is available 24/7, possesses a nearly infinite repository of knowledge, and never gets tired of answering your questions. That mentor is an AI.

Using AI as your personal tutor is perhaps the single most powerful way to accelerate your professional development. This aligns perfectly with the findings of the Stanford HAI study, which revealed that one of the primary desires among workers is for AI to be a tool for learning and skill development.[75] People want to get better at their jobs, and AI is an unprecedented resource for making that happen.

The most effective way to use AI as a tutor is to ask it to simplify complex concepts. Imagine you are a new marketing associate in your first week, and you are sitting in a meeting where your colleagues are discussing "programmatic advertising," "demand-side platforms," and "real-time bidding."

Instead of nodding along in confusion and hoping to figure it out later, you can open a private window on your laptop and ask an AI: "Explain programmatic advertising to me like I'm a 10-year-old." The AI will break down the complex jargon into a simple, easy-to-understand analogy, perhaps comparing it to an automated stock exchange for digital ads. You can then engage in a Socratic dialogue with the AI to deepen your understanding. You might ask, "What's the difference between a DSP and an SSP?" or "Walk me through the steps of a real-time bidding auction." You can continue this process, asking increasingly specific questions ("What are the most common metrics for measuring the success of a programmatic campaign?") until you have a solid foundational understanding. This allows you to learn in real time, without interrupting the flow of the meeting or revealing your lack of knowledge to your new colleagues.

This approach is not just for on-the-fly learning; it is also a powerful tool for deliberate upskilling. You can use AI to create a personalized learning plan. For example, you could give it a prompt like: "I am a junior financial analyst and I want to improve my financial modeling skills in Excel. I already know how to do basic formulas and pivot tables, but I want to learn how to build a three-statement model from scratch. Can you create a week-by-week learning plan for me? For each week, please include the key concepts to learn, the specific Excel functions to master, and links to high-quality online tutorials and resources. Also, suggest a small practice project for each week to reinforce the learning." The AI will generate a structured, actionable plan that you can follow at your own pace. It might suggest that Week 1 focuses on understanding the connections between the income statement, balance sheet, and cash flow statement. Week 2 might focus on mastering functions like XLOOKUP and INDEX/MATCH. Week 3 could be dedicated to building a simple discounted cash flow (DCF) model. This transforms a vague goal like "get better at Excel" into a concrete project plan.

This method of using AI as a learning tool is rapidly moving from a clever hack to a mainstream educational strategy. At the prestigious Wharton School of the University of Pennsylvania, Professor Ethan Mollick now requires all of his students to use AI in his courses. He sees it as an "intelligent collaborator" that can level the playing field, providing every student with a personal tutor to help them master difficult concepts. He argues that in an age of AI, the focus of education must shift from the memorization of information (a task at which AI excels) to the higher-order skills of critical thinking, problem-solving, and application.[76]

This shift is also happening at the K-12 level. In 2023, New York City public schools, the largest school district in the United States, reversed its ban on ChatGPT. The schools chancellor, David C. Banks, explained the decision by stating that the district was committed to "embracing the potential of this new technology to support our students and staff."[77] The message is clear: the educational establishment is beginning to recognize AI not as a tool for cheating, but as a powerful aid for learning. For an early-career professional, this is a game-changer. It means you are no longer limited by the formal training your company provides or the availability of your manager. You have the ability to take control of your own learning and development, to fill your knowledge gaps, and to build new skills on demand.

Section 2: AI as Your Productivity Engine

Beyond its role as a tutor, AI is a formidable engine for boosting your personal productivity. By automating the low-value, time-consuming tasks that often bog down an entry-level role, you can free up your time and mental energy to focus on the more challenging and visible projects that will help you advance.

One of the most immediate ways to leverage AI is for communication tasks. We all spend a significant portion of our day reading and writing emails. An AI can dramatically reduce this time. You can paste a long, convoluted email thread into an AI and ask it to "summarize the key action items and deadlines from this conversation." Instead of spending ten minutes reading through the back-and-forth, you get a concise summary in seconds. Similarly, when you need to write a professional email, you can give the AI a few bullet points and ask it to "draft a polite and professional email to a client confirming our meeting for next Tuesday at 10 AM and outlining the following agenda items." The AI will generate a well-structured draft that you can quickly edit and send. You can even ask it to adjust the tone: "Make this draft more formal," or "Rewrite this to be more friendly and concise."

This extends to all forms of writing. An AI can be your personal writing assistant, helping you overcome the intimidating blank page. If you need to write a report, a blog post, or a project proposal, you can start by asking the AI to generate an outline. Once you have the structure, you can ask it to write a first draft of a specific section. The key is to treat this as a starting point, not a final product. The AI's draft will likely be generic, but it provides you with raw material that you can then edit, refine, and infuse with your own voice and insights.

This process of partnering with the AI, using it for brainstorming, outlining, and drafting, is far more efficient than trying to create a perfect first draft from scratch.

For those in more technical roles, AI coding assistants like GitHub Copilot are transforming the way software is developed. These tools can autocomplete lines of code, suggest entire functions based on a simple comment, and even help debug errors by explaining what a piece of code is doing in plain English. One study found that junior employees using an AI assistant were able to complete tasks up to 1.5 hours faster than their peers who were not using the tool.[78] This allows them to learn more quickly and contribute to more complex projects earlier in their careers. It also helps them tackle one of the most common challenges for a new developer: understanding a large, existing codebase. They can highlight a section of unfamiliar code and ask the AI to explain its purpose and dependencies.

A now-famous anecdote from the tech world illustrates the power of AI as a performance equalizer. A company hired an intern who, by his own admission, was "grossly unqualified" for the role. He used AI tools extensively to help him with his coding tasks, asking the AI to explain concepts, debug his code, and suggest more efficient solutions. He performed so well that he was offered a full-time position. While his approach raises some ethical questions that we will address in the next section, his story demonstrates the incredible leverage that AI can provide, allowing a motivated but inexperienced individual to perform at a level far beyond their formal qualifications.[79]

The range of productivity-boosting applications is vast. You can use AI to take notes during a meeting (many video conferencing tools now have this feature built-in), to brainstorm ideas for a new project ("Give me 10 unconventional marketing ideas for a new brand of sustainable coffee"), to translate a document into another language, or to create a first draft of a presentation. The common thread is that in each case, the AI is handling the initial, time-consuming, and often low-value part of the task, allowing you to focus your human intelligence on the higher-level work of strategy, refinement, and critical thinking.

Section 3: Ethical Boundaries and the Rise of AI Fluency

With this great power comes great responsibility. As you begin to integrate AI into your daily work, it is absolutely vital that you understand and respect the ethical boundaries and company policies that govern its use. Failure to do so can have serious consequences for your career and your employer.

The first and most important rule is to protect sensitive information. Publicly available AI models like ChatGPT are not secure, private environments. The data you enter into them can be used to train future versions of the model and may even be reviewed by the company's employees. This means you should never paste confidential company data, proprietary code, or personal information about customers or colleagues into a public AI tool. Doing so is a major security breach that could lead to disciplinary action or even termination. Many companies are now deploying their own internal, secure versions of these AI tools, often called enterprise-grade or private instances. You must understand your company's specific policy and use only the approved tools for any work involving sensitive data.

The second ethical boundary is plagiarism and intellectual honesty. Using AI to help you brainstorm, outline, or write a first draft is a smart productivity strategy. Copying and pasting the AI's output verbatim and presenting it as your own work is plagiarism, plain and simple. You must always take the raw output from an AI and make it your own. This means editing it for accuracy, refining the language to match your own voice, adding your own unique insights, and verifying any factual claims the AI makes. The AI is your assistant, not your replacement. The final work product must be a reflection of your own thinking and effort. Think of it this way: if you hired a research assistant to gather information for a report, you would not put their name on the final document. You would use their research to inform your own analysis and writing. The same principle applies to AI.

Navigating these boundaries is a key component of a new core competency that is rapidly becoming a baseline expectation in the professional world: AI fluency. In the 1990s, computer literacy became a requirement for most office jobs. In the 2000s, proficiency with tools like Microsoft Excel became a standard skill. Today, AI fluency is the new "Excel literacy." It is the ability to effectively and ethically use AI tools to enhance your performance.

AI fluency can be broken down into four key sub-skills. The first is Prompt Crafting, the ability to ask clear, specific, and context-rich questions to get the best possible output from an AI. The second is Tool Selection, knowing which AI tool is right for which task. A large language model is great for writing, but an image generation model is needed for creating visuals. The third is Output Verification, the critical habit of never blindly trusting an AI's output. This means fact-checking its claims, reviewing its logic, and being aware of its potential for bias and hallucination.

The fourth is Ethical Application, having a firm grasp of the privacy and plagiarism rules that govern AI use in a professional setting.

The demand for this new skill is exploding. A 2025 recruiter survey found that AI-related skills are the fastest-growing category of requirements in job descriptions.[80] Companies are actively seeking out candidates who are not just aware of AI, but who can demonstrate a practical ability to use it. This means that learning to work with AI is no longer just a way to get ahead; it is becoming a prerequisite for getting in the door. By developing your AI fluency, you signal to employers that you are a modern, adaptable, and productive professional who is ready to contribute from day one.

Conclusion

The arrival of the machine colleague has fundamentally changed the expectations for early-career professionals. It is no longer enough to simply show up and learn on the job in a passive way. You are now expected to be a proactive, self-directed learner and a highly productive contributor from day one. AI is the tool that makes this possible. By embracing AI as your personal tutor, you can accelerate your learning curve and master new skills at an unprecedented pace. By leveraging it as your productivity engine, you can automate the drudgery and focus on high-impact work that gets you noticed.

This new way of working requires a new core competency: AI fluency. This is not just a technical skill; it is a strategic mindset. It is about understanding how to partner with intelligent machines to augment your own abilities, while always operating within a strong ethical framework. Mastering this skill is no longer optional. It is a fundamental requirement for building a successful career in the 21st century.

Using AI for personal learning and productivity is the first and most important step. But to truly stand out and build a resilient career, you must go beyond simply using the tools for your own benefit. You must use them to create tangible, demonstrable proof of your skills. The next chapter will show you how to do just that.

Chapter 7: Projects, Portfolios & Proof of Work

Introduction

In the face of career disruption, there are two ways to react: with anxiety or with action. Kye, a recent graduate, chose action. After losing his job, he found himself, like millions of others, facing the demoralizing task of writing endless, customized cover letters for countless job applications. He recognized the process for what it was: a repetitive, soul-crushing form of drudgery. But instead of just grinding through it, he saw an opportunity. He asked himself a powerful question: could this problem be solved with technology? Using accessible, no-code tools, he built a simple web application he called CoverDoc.ai. The tool allowed users to upload their resume and a job description, and it would generate a tailored first draft of a cover letter. It was a direct, creative response to a personal pain point. His project was not just a clever idea; it was the ultimate form of proof. It demonstrated his resilience, his problem-solving skills, and his ability to create value out of thin air.[81]

Kye's story is the perfect embodiment of the new imperative in the modern job market. We are in the midst of a credibility crisis for the traditional resume. As we have established, AI tools have made it trivially easy for anyone to generate a flawless-sounding, keyword-optimized resume and cover letter. The result is a flood of applications that are polished, professional, and almost completely interchangeable. For a hiring manager, this creates a profound problem of signal versus noise. When everyone sounds perfect, how do you identify the truly capable candidates? The answer is that you stop relying on what people claim they can do and start looking for what they have actually done.

This is the shift from a resume-first to a proof-of-work-first mindset. In a world where AI can generate claims but not proof, your portfolio of projects becomes your most valuable career asset. It is the tangible evidence of your abilities, a compelling narrative of your curiosity, your skills, and your capacity to get things done. This chapter is your guide to building that proof. We will demystify the process of creating projects, even for those with no technical background. We will explore what hiring managers are desperately looking for in a sea of generic applications. And we will introduce a powerful strategy for amplifying your work to ensure it gets seen by the right people. It is time to move beyond simply claiming you have skills and start proving it.

Section 1: "Vibe Coding" and the No-Code Revolution

For many people, the idea of building a project is immediately intimidating. It conjures up images of complex code, technical jargon, and years of specialized training. This psychological barrier is often the biggest obstacle to getting started. But this perception is rapidly becoming outdated. The rise of a new generation of powerful, user-friendly tools has democratized the act of creation, making it possible for anyone with a good idea and a willingness to learn to build impressive projects. This new approach has been playfully dubbed "vibe coding" by Andrej Karpathy, a prominent AI researcher. He defines it as a process where you are "intensely familiar with the data" and have a clear vision of what you want to achieve, but you use high-level, intuitive tools (including AI itself) to handle the technical execution.[82]

The core idea of vibe coding is to focus on the what and the why, not just the how. It is a liberating mindset that frees you from the need to be a technical expert in every layer of the stack. You do not need to know how to write Python code from scratch to analyze a dataset. You can use an AI tool to write the code for you, as long as you have the critical thinking skills to define the problem, interpret the results, and spot any errors. This shifts the emphasis from rote technical knowledge to the more valuable skills of strategic thinking and problem-solving. It is an active demonstration of the C.H.A.T. model in practice: you use your Creativity to come up with the project idea, your critical Thinking to guide the process, and your Adaptability to learn the new tools required to bring it to life.

This new reality is powered by the no-code and low-code revolution. An entire ecosystem of platforms has emerged that allows you to build sophisticated applications, websites, and automations using simple drag-and-drop interfaces and natural language prompts. These tools are the building blocks for your first portfolio project.

Consider a tool like Zapier. At its core, Zapier is a digital switchboard that allows you to connect different web applications and make them work together. You can create automated workflows, or "Zaps," based on simple "if this, then that" logic. Imagine you are a student applying for internships. You could create a Zap to streamline your process. The workflow might be: "When I save a new job posting to a specific folder in my Google Drive (the trigger), automatically create a new card in

Trello with a checklist of application tasks (Action 1), set a deadline reminder in my Google Calendar for one week from today (Action 2), and add a new row to a Google Sheet to track my applications (Action 3)." Building this does not require a single line of code, yet it solves a real problem (managing a complex job search) and demonstrates your ability to think systematically and leverage modern tools. It is a perfect, simple, and highly effective first project.

For more complex projects, platforms like Replit or Bubble are excellent starting points. Replit is an online coding environment that makes it incredibly easy to start programming in various languages, often with AI assistance to help you along the way. Bubble is a powerful no-code platform that allows you to build fully functional web applications, complete with user accounts, databases, and complex workflows, all through a visual interface. Using a tool like Bubble, you could build a simple project management app for your personal use, a directory of local volunteer opportunities, or a tool to track your job applications. The process of building such an application will teach you invaluable skills about product design, user experience, and logical thinking, all without the steep learning curve of traditional programming.

The key to getting started is to think small and solve a problem you personally have. The most common mistake people make is trying to build something massive and world-changing for their first project. This often leads to overwhelm and abandonment. Instead, look for a small, annoying, repetitive task in your own life. Is there a piece of information you wish was easier to track? Is there a manual process you could automate? Start there. The goal of your first project is not to build a billion-dollar startup; it is to learn, to create something tangible, and to have a compelling story to tell. By embracing the mindset of vibe coding and leveraging the power of no-code tools, you can begin building your portfolio today, regardless of your technical background.

Section 2: What Hiring Managers Want to See

The shift from resumes to portfolios is one of the most significant changes in the modern hiring landscape. As we discussed in the previous chapter, recruiters are drowning in a sea of AI-optimized applications that are becoming increasingly difficult to differentiate. Imagine the daily reality of a corporate recruiter: a small screen, a queue of hundreds of PDF resumes, and a few seconds to make a judgment on each one. In this environment of information overload, a generic list of skills and responsibilities begins to blur into a meaningless fog. This has led to a growing skepticism of the resume as a reliable signal of a candidate's true abilities. In response, hiring managers are desperately seeking authentic, undeniable proof of skill.

A popular hiring newsletter for the tech industry recently advised its readers to prioritize a candidate's projects over their GPA, arguing that a real-world project is a far better predictor of on-the-job performance than academic credentials. A recruiter quoted in a 2025 industry report captured this sentiment perfectly: "I ask for the GitHub or the results."[83] They want to see your code, your designs, your writing, your analysis. They want to see what you have actually done.

So, what makes a good portfolio project? It is not necessarily about technical complexity. A simple project that is well-executed and thoughtfully documented is far more impressive than a complex one that is sloppy and poorly explained. A compelling project generally has three key characteristics.

First, it solves a real problem. The problem does not have to be world-changing, but it should be genuine. The CoverDoc.ai project is a perfect example. It solved a real, relatable problem that the creator himself was experiencing. This demonstrates an entrepreneurial mindset and an ability to see the world through the eyes of a user, a valuable skill in any role. A generic project, like another "To-Do List App," is far less impressive than a specific one, like a "Roommate Chore-Tracking App that Sends Automated Reminders." The latter shows that you can identify a specific pain point in a specific context and design a solution for it. Your project could be a tool that automates a tedious task for a student club you are in, a data analysis that provides a new insight into a local community issue, or a website that helps you and your friends organize your weekly game night. The scope is less important than the fact that it is grounded in a real-world need.

Second, it demonstrates curiosity and a willingness to learn. Your portfolio should tell the story of your growth. A great project is one that clearly pushes you outside of your comfort zone. In your project documentation, you should be open about the challenges you faced and how you overcame them. Did you have to learn a new tool? Did you run into an unexpected bug that took you hours to solve? Did your initial idea fail, forcing you to pivot? Sharing this part of the process is not a sign of weakness; it is a powerful signal of resilience and adaptability, two of the most sought-after skills in the C.H.A.T. model. It shows a hiring manager that you are not afraid of a challenge and that you are committed to continuous learning. Including a section in your case study titled "What I Learned" or "Challenges and Solutions" is a powerful way to frame this narrative.

Third, it is well-documented. A project without a good explanation is just a link. The documentation is where you connect the dots for the hiring manager and tell the story of your work. Every project in your portfolio should be presented as a mini case study. This write-up should be clear, concise, and structured. A good model is to use the STAR method that we discussed for interviews. Begin by explaining the Situation or Problem you were trying to solve. Then, describe the Task you set for yourself. Detail the Action you took, including the tools you used and the process you followed. Include screenshots, simple user flow diagrams, or snippets of code to make your process tangible. Finally, and most importantly, share the Result. What was the outcome of your project? Did you achieve your goal? What did you learn from the process? A great case study also includes a section on "Future Improvements," where you discuss what you would do differently or what features you would add next. This demonstrates strategic thinking and a commitment to iterative improvement. This structured narrative makes it easy for a busy recruiter to quickly understand the value of your work.

Section 3: Portfolio Stacking: Amplifying Your Work

Creating a great project is the first step. Ensuring that it gets seen and understood by the right people is the second. To do this, you need to think like a marketer and adopt a strategy of "portfolio stacking." The core idea is that a single project should not just result in a single portfolio piece. It should be turned into a stack of multiple, interconnected assets, each designed for a different audience and a different platform. This approach dramatically increases the visibility of your work and demonstrates a sophisticated understanding of professional communication.

Let's walk through an example. Imagine you have completed the data analysis project we discussed in the last chapter: "How I Used Public Transit Data to Find the Best Place for a New Coffee Shop in My City." Here is how you could "stack" this project to maximize its impact.

Layer 1: The Project Itself

This is the foundation of your stack. It is the raw proof of your technical work. In this case, it might be a GitHub repository containing your Python code, the raw data files, and a clean, well-commented Jupyter Notebook that walks through your analysis step by step. For a design project, this would be the high-fidelity mockups in a Figma file. For a no-code application, it would be the live, working app. This layer is for the deeply technical reviewer who wants to see the nuts and bolts of your work.

Layer 2: The Portfolio Case Study

This is the definitive, detailed write-up of your project, hosted on your personal website or portfolio page. This is where you use the STAR method to tell the full story. You would start with the problem statement, detail your process with screenshots and diagrams, and present your results with compelling charts and a final recommendation. This case study is your primary sales document, designed for the hiring manager who is seriously evaluating your candidacy. It is the link you put at the top of your resume.

Layer 3: The Blog Post

This asset is a more narrative, less formal version of your case study, published on a platform like Medium or LinkedIn. The tone should be more conversational and focused on the key insights. The title might be something like, "What I Learned About My City by Analyzing 1 Million Bus Rides." In this post, you would focus less on the technical details and more on the interesting story that the data revealed. This piece is designed for a broader audience. Its purpose is discoverability and thought leadership. A well-written blog post, optimized with relevant keywords, can show up in search results and attract "inbound" interest from recruiters and other professionals in your field who might not have otherwise seen your portfolio.

Layer 4: The Social Media Snippet

This is the top layer of your stack, designed to capture attention in a fast-moving social media feed. You could create a short video for TikTok or YouTube Shorts that quickly walks through your project, showing the most interesting data visualization. You could create a thread on X (formerly Twitter) or a carousel post on LinkedIn that breaks down your project into a series of bite-sized insights, with each post linking back to the full blog post or case study. This layer is your marketing campaign. It is the hook that draws people in and encourages them to explore the deeper layers of your work.

This strategy is not just for technical projects. A marketing student could do a deep-dive analysis of a successful brand's social media strategy. Layer 1 would be the detailed report itself, perhaps as a well-designed PDF. Layer 2 would be the portfolio case study summarizing the project. Layer 3 would be a LinkedIn article on the "Top 3 Lessons from Brand X's Marketing Genius." Layer 4 would be a series of visually engaging carousel posts on LinkedIn or Instagram highlighting the key findings. By adopting this portfolio stacking strategy, you demonstrate a set of skills that go far beyond the technical. You show that you can not only do the work, but that you can also communicate the value of the work to different audiences, a critical skill in any professional role.

Conclusion

In an AI-driven job market where anyone can generate a plausible-sounding resume, your portfolio is your ultimate differentiator. It is the undeniable, tangible proof of your skills, your curiosity, and your ability to create value. It is the story that no AI can write for you. The rise of no-code tools and the "vibe coding" mindset has made the act of creation more accessible than ever before. You do not need to be a traditional programmer to build something meaningful. You just need a problem to solve and the initiative to get started. By creating projects that are grounded in real-world needs, that showcase your learning process, and that are documented with clear, compelling case studies, you can build a body of work that speaks for itself. And by using the portfolio stacking strategy to amplify that work, you can ensure that your story is heard. This is how you move from being a passive applicant to an active creator, taking control of your own career narrative.

Now that you know how to prove your skills with a portfolio, the next chapter will provide a comprehensive playbook for becoming a true AI power user. We will explore the daily habits, the mental models, and the specific techniques you can use to supercharge your learning, amplify your productivity, and build even more impressive projects to add to your stack.

Chapter 8: The AI Power User Playbook

Introduction

There are two types of professionals in the AI-integrated workplace: the casual user and the power user. The casual user dabbles. They might ask ChatGPT to write a funny poem for a colleague's birthday or use it to get a quick answer to a trivia question. They see AI as a novelty, a clever toy that is occasionally useful. For them, AI is a peripheral tool, something to be used sporadically when a specific, simple need arises. Their interaction is transactional and shallow. The power user, on the other hand, is a strategist. They see AI not as a toy, but as a lever, a fundamental part of their professional toolkit that is as indispensable as email or a spreadsheet. They have moved beyond simple queries and are actively integrating AI into their daily workflows, using it to learn faster, think better, and automate the drudgery that holds them back. They are the ones who are truly building the AI Advantage.

This chapter is your tactical guide to making that leap. It is the playbook for moving from casual experimentation to sophisticated, strategic application. The practices outlined here are designed to help you achieve the ideal human-AI partnership that the Stanford HAI study identified as the ultimate goal for so many professionals: a collaboration where the machine handles the tedious work and accelerates learning, freeing you to focus on the high-value, uniquely human contributions that define your career.[84] This is not about becoming a programmer or a data scientist. It is about developing a new set of habits and mental models that will make you a more effective and indispensable professional in any field. This is how you go from being a consumer of AI to a wielder of it.

Section 1: The Five Strategic Practices for AI Fluency

Becoming a power user is not a single event; it is a continuous process built on a foundation of consistent habits. It is more like developing a fitness routine than passing a one-time exam. This section breaks down that process into five strategic practices. By deliberately incorporating these practices into your professional life, you can systematically build your AI fluency and transform your relationship with this powerful technology from one of passive curiosity to one of active partnership.

Practice 1: Build Your Foundation (Structured Learning)

You cannot effectively use a tool that you do not understand. The first and most important practice of an AI power user is to invest time in structured learning to build a solid foundational knowledge of what AI is, how it works, and what its capabilities and limitations are. This is not about learning to code machine learning models. It is about building the mental models you need to think strategically about the technology. Just as you do not need to be a mechanic to be a good driver, you do not need to be an AI engineer to be an AI power user. But you do need to understand the basic rules of the road, how to operate the vehicle safely, and what it is designed to do. Using a powerful AI without this foundational knowledge is like driving a sports car without knowing what the different pedals do; you are more likely to cause a crash than to get where you are going.

For the non-technical professional, the goal is to grasp a few key concepts. You should understand the difference between traditional programming (where a human writes explicit, step-by-step rules for the computer to follow) and machine learning (where the computer learns the rules by identifying patterns in vast amounts of data). You should have a basic understanding of what a large language model (LLM) is, a complex neural network trained on a massive corpus of text and other data, and how that training process shapes its abilities. Most importantly, you must be intimately familiar with its key limitations. You need to understand, on a deep level, that an LLM is a probabilistic text generator, not a factual database. It is designed to predict the next most likely word in a sequence, which is why it can generate such fluent and coherent text. It is also why it is prone to "hallucination", the tendency to invent facts, sources, and figures with complete confidence. Understanding this principle is the key to using the tool responsibly and avoiding embarrassing or dangerous errors.

Fortunately, there has been an explosion of high-quality, accessible courses designed specifically for this purpose. A perfect starting point is Coursera's "AI For Everyone," taught by Andrew Ng, one of the most respected figures in the field. This course is explicitly designed for a non-technical audience and provides a brilliant overview of AI terminology, concepts, and real-world applications. Another excellent, free option is Google's AI Essentials course, which offers a practical introduction to using generative AI tools in a professional context. These courses are designed to be completed in a few hours, but the return on that small investment of time is immense.

Committing to a structured course like one of these is a powerful first step. It provides a curated learning path that cuts through the noise and hype, giving you a solid framework for understanding everything else you will learn about AI. Think of it as the prerequisite for all the other practices in this playbook. It is the investment you make in building the vocabulary and the conceptual understanding to use these tools with confidence and sophistication.

Practice 2: Curate Your Information Stack (Daily Habits)

The field of artificial intelligence is moving at a dizzying pace. A new model, a new tool, or a new technique seems to emerge every week. The sheer volume of news, research papers, and opinion pieces is overwhelming. Trying to keep up with everything is a recipe for burnout and information overload. The power user does not try to drink from the firehose. Instead, they carefully curate a personal information stack, a small, manageable set of high-quality resources that they engage with as a regular habit. This practice is about building a system for ambient learning, allowing you to stay current without being overwhelmed. It is about finding the signal in the noise.

Your information stack should be a mix of different formats that fit your learning style. For daily updates on the latest news and tool releases, a few well-chosen newsletters are invaluable. Ben's Bites is a popular choice, offering a quick, scannable summary of the day's most important AI news in a format that can be read in five minutes. The Neuron provides a slightly deeper dive, with clear explanations of new research and trends, often breaking down complex topics into easy-to-understand language. Subscribing to just one or two of these and spending ten minutes reading them each morning with your coffee is a highly efficient way to stay on the cutting edge.

For deeper, more contextual understanding, podcasts are an excellent resource. They can be integrated into your commute, your workout, or your household chores. In Machines We Trust, from the MIT Technology Review, offers well-researched stories on the real-world impact of AI, exploring both its promise and its peril. Latent Space is a more technical podcast that features in-depth interviews with the researchers and engineers who are building the next generation of AI systems. Even if you do not understand every technical detail, listening to these conversations will give you a powerful sense of where the field is heading and what the people on the front lines are thinking about.

To round out your stack, it is useful to follow a few key thinkers on social media platforms like X (formerly Twitter) or LinkedIn. People like Professor Ethan Mollick of Wharton or Andrew Ng of Coursera often share real-time insights, practical experiments, and links to important new research. Following a curated list of five to ten such experts can provide a valuable stream of high-signal information.

The key to this practice is curation and consistency. Do not subscribe to twenty newsletters and a dozen podcasts. Choose two or three of each that you genuinely find valuable and commit to engaging with them regularly. Use a "read-it-later" app like Pocket or Instapaper to save interesting articles you come across during the day, and set aside a specific time each week to read them. This habit of consistent, low-intensity learning will compound over time, building your knowledge base and ensuring that you are never caught off guard by a major shift in the technological landscape.

Practice 3: Make GPT-4 Your Co-worker (Workflow Integration)

This is where theory meets practice. The true power user does not just know about AI; they actively use it, every single day, as an integrated part of their professional workflow. The goal is to develop a seamless partnership with a powerful AI assistant like GPT-4, treating it not as a search engine, but as an intelligent, versatile co-worker. This means moving beyond simple, one-shot queries and learning to use the AI in a variety of roles.

- **AI as Your Research Assistant**: A powerful AI can dramatically accelerate the process of research and synthesis. Instead of spending hours reading through dense articles or reports, you can use the AI to do the initial pass. You can give it a link to a long academic paper and ask it to "summarize the key findings of this study and explain its methodology in simple terms." You can provide it with a dozen articles on a topic and ask it to "act as a market research analyst. Analyze these articles and identify the three main arguments for and against this position, and list the key evidence cited by each side." This does not replace the need for you to read the source material, but it provides you with a powerful summary and a mental map of the landscape, allowing you to conduct your own deep dive with much greater efficiency.

- **AI as Your Sounding Board**: One of the most valuable things a good colleague can do is provide a second opinion. An AI can be a surprisingly effective sparring partner for your ideas. Before you send an important email, you can paste the draft into the AI and ask, "Critique this email. Is the tone professional? Is the call to action clear? How could it be improved?" Before a big presentation, you can outline your argument and ask the AI to "act as a skeptical CEO and ask me three tough questions about this proposal." A consulting manager at a major firm described how he uses GPT-4 as a constant thought partner, helping him to refine his strategies and anticipate client objections. This process of externalizing and testing your ideas, often called "red teaming," can dramatically improve the quality of your work by forcing you to confront potential weaknesses in your arguments before you present them to a human audience.

- **AI as Your Creativity Partner**: While AI may not possess true creativity, it is a phenomenal tool for augmenting our own. It can be a powerful antidote to the blank page. If you are stuck for ideas, you can use it as a brainstorming partner. For example: "I'm writing a blog post about the importance of project portfolios for early-career professionals. Give me 10 unconventional headlines for this post." The AI might generate a list of ideas, most of which will be generic, but one or two might contain a spark of an interesting angle you had not considered. You can also use it to generate analogies to explain complex topics or to rewrite a dense paragraph in a more engaging and accessible style.

- **AI as Your On-Demand Tutor**: As we discussed in the previous chapter, AI is a phenomenal learning tool. The power user makes this a daily habit. Whenever you encounter a concept you do not understand, your first instinct should be to ask the AI to explain it. This could be a technical term, a business concept, or a historical event. By using the AI to constantly fill in your knowledge gaps, you can engage in a process of continuous, real-time learning that is perfectly tailored to your needs.

Integrating AI into your workflow in these ways requires a shift in mindset. It is about developing the habit of asking, "Could an AI help me with this?" for every task you face. Over time, this partnership becomes second nature, a seamless collaboration that makes you a more knowledgeable, efficient, and effective professional.

Practice 4: Experiment with Agentic Workflows (Automation)

The next level of AI mastery involves moving from single-prompt interactions to orchestrating the AI to perform multi-step tasks. This is the practice of building "agentic workflows," where you are not just using the AI to complete a single step, but are designing a system where the AI, in combination with other tools, can carry out an entire process. This is how you truly begin to automate your own drudgery and free up your time for higher-value work.

The concept of an agentic workflow is simpler than it sounds. It is about connecting different applications together, with an AI often acting as the "brain" of the operation. The easiest way to get started with this is by using no-code automation platforms like Zapier, which we introduced in the last chapter.

A powerful real-world example of this comes from Zapier itself. The company built an automated workflow to handle customer support notifications. When a customer reported an issue, the system would automatically use an AI to analyze the problem, search the company's internal knowledge base for a potential solution, and then draft a personalized response to the customer. This single workflow saved the company an estimated $1 million in support costs.[85]

While that is a large-scale corporate example, you can apply the exact same principles to your own personal productivity. Imagine you want to automate the process of tracking industry news. You could build a simple agentic workflow in Zapier:

1. **Trigger**: When a new article is published on a specific RSS feed (e.g., a major industry blog).
2. **Action 1**: Send the content of the article to GPT-4 with a prompt to "summarize this article into three key bullet points."
3. **Action 2**: Take the summary from GPT-4 and send it as a direct message to yourself in Slack.

This simple, two-step workflow, which can be built in minutes with no code, creates a personalized, automated news summary service. By experimenting with these kinds of simple automations, you begin to develop a new way of thinking. You start to see your work not as a series of manual tasks, but as a system of processes, many of which can be automated. This mindset shift, from being a doer of tasks to a designer of systems, is a significant step up in professional maturity.

Practice 5: Adopt a "Side Quest" Mindset (Continuous Growth)

The final practice of the AI power user is to adopt a mindset of continuous, project-based learning. The field of AI is moving too quickly for your knowledge to ever be static. The only way to keep up is to be constantly learning by doing. This is the "side quest" mindset. It is about proactively taking on small, low-stakes projects for the express purpose of learning a new skill or experimenting with a new tool.

The "side quest" framing is psychologically powerful because it lowers the stakes. This is not your main job, a career-defining project with a tight deadline and a high risk of failure. It is a fun, curiosity-driven experiment. This makes it much easier to get started and much less painful to fail, and failure is an inevitable and valuable part of the learning process.

A great example of this in practice is the #100DaysOfAI challenge, a popular movement in the online tech community. Participants publicly commit to spending a small amount of time each day for 100 days learning something new about AI and sharing their progress. This could be anything from learning a new prompting technique to building a simple AI-powered application. The public commitment creates accountability, and the daily habit builds momentum.

You can apply this mindset in your own career. A new hire at a finance company, for example, noticed that his team was spending hours each week manually compiling data for a weekly report. As a side quest, he spent a few evenings learning how to use a simple scripting language with AI assistance to automate the process. He built a small tool that pulled the data from various sources and generated the report automatically. When he shared it with his manager, he was not just seen as a competent new hire; he was seen as a proactive problem-solver and an innovator. His side quest created tangible value for the team and served as a powerful piece of proof of work for his own career.

These side quests are the engine that feeds your portfolio. They are the raw material for the case studies and projects we discussed in the last chapter. Adopting a side quest mindset is about cultivating a state of active curiosity. It is about seeing your job not just as a set of assigned tasks, but as a playground for experimentation and learning. The power user is never content with their current skill set. They are always looking for the next side quest, the next opportunity to learn, to build, and to grow.

Conclusion: The Weekly Challenge Planner

Becoming a power user can feel like a daunting goal. The five practices outlined in this chapter, structured learning, curating an information stack, workflow integration, experimenting with automation, and adopting a side quest mindset, are powerful, but they only work if you apply them consistently. To help you turn these ideas into action, this playbook concludes with a simple but effective tool: the Weekly Challenge Planner.

The planner is a simple template that you can use at the beginning of each week to set a small, achievable goal related to each of the five practices. It is a way to turn a vague intention like "I should learn more about AI" into a concrete, actionable plan. It is a system for building habits. Your planner for a given week might look something like this:

- **Practice 1 (Foundation)**: Complete one module of the Google AI Essentials course.
- **Practice 2 (Curation)**: Read The Neuron newsletter three times this week.
- **Practice 3 (Integration)**: Use GPT-4 to help me outline the monthly report.
- **Practice 4 (Automation)**: Build one simple, two-step Zap to automate a personal task.

- **Practice 5 (Side Quest)**: Spend one hour experimenting with a new AI image generation tool.

The goals are small, specific, and measurable. By breaking down the larger goal of becoming a power user into these weekly challenges, you can build momentum and turn these practices into durable habits. This is the key to sustainable, long-term growth.

The skills you build by following this playbook are the foundation for a resilient and future-proof career. They will make you more effective, more adaptable, and more valuable in any role you take on. With these skills, you are now ready to tackle the more complex challenges faced by professionals who are already established in their careers. The next part of the book will provide a dedicated playbook for mid-career professionals looking to adapt and advance in the age of AI.

PART III: ADAPT AND ADVANCE: FOR MID-CAREER PROFESSIONALS

Chapter 9: Is My Job Safe?

Introduction

A manager in sales and customer service shared a story that perfectly illustrates the quiet, creeping nature of AI-driven disruption. At the start of 2024, he began encouraging his team to embrace AI, anticipating that the repetitive administrative tasks that consumed their days would become obsolete within a few years. His goal was to shift their focus toward higher-level strategy and communication, the kind of work that builds lasting customer relationships. In January, he recalled, this idea was met with "skepticism and funny faces." By October, the skepticism had vanished. New AI features integrated into their customer relationship management (CRM) software could now analyze incoming emails, compare them to past orders, and generate detailed draft responses, complete with article numbers, pricing, and availability. The change was not a dramatic layoff announcement; it was a software update. The manager noted that the team's attitude had "noticeably changed."[86] The future he had been warning them about had arrived, not with a bang, but with a new button in their user interface.

This is the reality of "creep risk." For most mid-career professionals, the threat of AI is not a sudden, cataclysmic event, but a gradual erosion of the tasks that once defined their roles. It is the slow but steady automation of the routine, the predictable, and the administrative. This form of change can be more insidious than a mass layoff because it often goes unnoticed until it is too late. It is the feeling of your professional ground slowly turning to sand beneath your feet. This chapter is designed to move you from a state of vague anxiety to one of clear-eyed awareness. We will explore the subtle signals of disruption that are already appearing across industries. We will then provide a step-by-step guide to conducting a "Creep Risk" Audit on your own role, a powerful tool for identifying your specific vulnerabilities. Finally, we will examine the warning signs of a brittle career model, helping you to see the bigger picture of your professional resilience. The question "Is my job safe?" is no longer the right one. The better question is, "How is my job changing, and am I prepared to evolve with it?"

Section 1: The Subtle Signals of Disruption

Job disruption in the age of AI rarely happens overnight. It is a process, not an event. It begins with subtle signals, small shifts in workflow and technology that, over time, accumulate into a fundamental transformation of a role or even an entire department. Understanding these early warning signs is the first step toward proactive adaptation. The experiences of companies across different sectors provide a clear picture of what this process looks like in practice, revealing two primary paths: outright replacement and strategic evolution.

Consider the case of Dukaan, an e-commerce platform in India. In a move that made international headlines, the company replaced approximately 90 percent of its customer support staff with a sophisticated AI chatbot. The results, from a purely business perspective, were dramatic. The time it took to provide an initial response to a customer query dropped from just under two minutes to instantaneous. The time to fully resolve a customer's issue was slashed from over two hours to just over three minutes. And the cost of customer support was reduced by a staggering 85 percent.[87] For the company, it was a massive efficiency gain. For the employees whose jobs were eliminated, it was a stark demonstration of how quickly a human-centric role can be automated when the tasks are sufficiently repetitive and rule-based. The work of a first-line support agent often involves answering a limited set of common questions, a pattern-matching exercise at which AI excels. The Dukaan story is a cautionary tale that illustrates the high-risk end of the disruption spectrum.

Disruption can also take a more nuanced form, leading not to elimination but to evolution. The Swedish retailer IKEA offers a compelling example of this alternative path. Like many large companies, IKEA is investing heavily in AI to handle first-line customer support. An executive described their new AI, nicknamed "Billie," as the primary point of contact for most customer queries. However, instead of laying off the call center employees whose tasks were being automated, IKEA is strategically upskilling them. The company is retraining these employees to become interior design consultants, leveraging their deep product knowledge and customer service skills in a more creative and advisory capacity.[88]

This is a profoundly important model. It shows a company that understands the difference between tasks and people. The task of answering a routine question about a product's dimensions is automatable. The person who performed that task, however, possesses valuable skills, communication, problem-solving, brand knowledge, that can be redeployed to a higher-value, more human-centric role that requires creativity and personalized advice. The IKEA case is not a story of replacement, but of role redesign. It is a strategic choice to move human capital up the value chain, from answering simple questions to solving complex customer problems.

These two case studies reveal the subtle signals you should be watching for in your own organization. The first signal is the introduction of new tools that begin to automate pieces of your workflow. This is the "creep" in creep risk. It might be a new feature in your CRM that drafts email responses, a new plugin in your spreadsheet software that automates data analysis, or a new internal AI that can summarize long documents. These tools are often introduced under the banner of "helping" you and making you more "efficient." While this is often true, you must also recognize them as indicators of which tasks your organization views as automatable.

The second signal is a shift in corporate language. Are leaders starting to talk more about "efficiency," "productivity," and "automation" in company-wide meetings and emails? Is there a new emphasis on data-driven decision-making and a push to quantify every aspect of performance? This linguistic shift often precedes a technological one.

The third signal is a change in the skills your company is hiring for or promoting. Are new roles emerging that require AI literacy? Are training programs being offered to upskill employees in data analysis or prompt engineering? Are the job descriptions for roles like yours starting to include phrases like "experience with AI tools preferred"? These are not necessarily signs of impending layoffs, but they are clear indicators that the ground is shifting beneath your feet. They are the early tremors that warn of a larger earthquake to come.

Section 2: The "Creep Risk" Audit: A Step-by-Step Guide

Awareness of the general trend is useful, but true preparation requires a specific, personal diagnosis. You need to move from understanding the abstract risk to understanding your risk. The "Creep Risk" Audit is a practical, step-by-step process for deconstructing your own role to identify your specific vulnerabilities and, more importantly, your areas of durable strength. This audit is framed by the core findings of the Stanford HAI study, which gives us a powerful lens for the analysis. The goal is not just to identify what can be automated, but to distinguish between the drudgery you would be happy to give up and the meaningful work that constitutes your Human Edge.

Step 1: Deconstruct Your Role into a Task Inventory

The first step is to create a granular inventory of your work. For one full week, keep a detailed log of every task you perform. Be ruthlessly specific. Do not just write "worked on the quarterly report." Break it down into its component tasks: "gathered sales data from Salesforce," "cleaned and formatted the data in Excel," "wrote the initial draft of the executive summary," "created charts and graphs to visualize the key trends," "collaborated with the finance team to verify the numbers," and "presented the findings to leadership." Do not just write "managed email." Instead, list the different types of email tasks: "responded to routine client inquiries," "scheduled internal meetings," "wrote project update emails," "negotiated a contract via email." The more detailed your list, the more insightful your audit will be. Aim for a list of at least 20 to 30 distinct weekly tasks.

Step 2: Apply the Stanford HAI Lens: Drudgery vs. Meaningful Work

Now, take your task inventory and create two columns. The first column is for "Drudgery." These are the tasks that are repetitive, tedious, and often feel like they get in the way of your "real" work. They are the tasks that drain your energy. The second column is for "Meaningful Work." These are the tasks that energize you, that require your unique skills and judgment, and that you believe create the most value. This is the work that, as the Stanford study found, is central to your professional identity.[89] Be honest with yourself. This step is about connecting your daily work to your sense of purpose and professional fulfillment. A task is likely "meaningful" if it allows you to use the skills of the C.H.A.T. model: your Creativity, your Humanity, your Adaptability, or your critical Thinking. A task is likely "drudgery" if it is a rote, predictable process that requires little of your unique human intelligence. The goal of this step is to create a clear picture of what you actually do all day, and how you feel about it. This reframes the audit from a purely negative exercise ("what's at risk?") to a more empowering one ("what do I want to protect and amplify?").

Step 3: Assess the Automation Potential of Each Task

This is the analytical core of the audit. Go through your task inventory, one item at a time, and assess its potential for automation by current AI technologies. To do this, think like a machine. Ask yourself a series of questions about each task: Does this task follow a clear set of rules? Is there a predictable input and a predictable output? Could I write a step-by-step instruction manual for a new hire to perform this task perfectly every time? If the answer to these questions is yes, the automation potential is high. Use the research as your guide.

- Is the task a routine administrative or clerical function, like scheduling, data entry, or form filling? Research shows that up to 46 percent of these tasks could be automated.[90]
- Is it a legal-support task, like reviewing contracts or summarizing depositions? Generative AI could handle an estimated 44 percent of these duties.[91]
- Is it a routine marketing task, like writing basic ad copy, creating simple visuals, or mining consumer data? These are all tasks that AI can now perform in minutes.[92]
- Does your role align with those identified in recent research as having high exposure? A Bloomberg analysis, for example, found that AI has the potential to automate 67 percent of a sales representative's tasks (like lead qualification and initial outreach) and 53 percent of a market research analyst's tasks (like data collection and initial analysis).[93]

For each task, assign a simple score: High, Medium, or Low potential for automation. A "High" score goes to tasks that are repetitive, rule-based, and involve processing structured data. A "Low" score goes to tasks that are novel, strategic, require complex interpersonal negotiation, or involve working in unpredictable physical environments.

Step 4: Synthesize Your Findings and Identify Your Risk Profile

The final step is to synthesize your results. Look at the tasks you have identified as having a high potential for automation. Are most of them in your "Drudgery" column? If so, this is a positive sign. It means that AI is poised to liberate you from the least enjoyable parts of your job, creating an opportunity for you to evolve your role. This is the IKEA model of augmentation. Your strategic goal should be to proactively seek out AI tools to automate this work, and then reinvest your newfound time in the tasks in your "Meaningful Work" column.

However, if you find that many of the tasks in your "Meaningful Work" column also have a high potential for automation, this is a significant warning sign. It suggests that the core of your current role is vulnerable, and you may be on a path closer to the Dukaan model of replacement. This is your creep risk score. A high score does not mean you are doomed, but it does mean that you need to act with urgency to develop new, less automatable skills.

Section 3: Warning Signs of a Brittle Career Model

The Creep Risk Audit provides a snapshot of your current role. The final piece of the analysis is to zoom out and assess the resilience of your overall career model. A "brittle" career is one that is highly susceptible to a single shock, like the rapid advance of a new technology. A resilient career, in contrast, is diversified and adaptable. There are two primary warning signs of a brittle career model.

The first warning sign is an over-reliance on a single, highly automatable skill. The IBM case study is a perfect illustration of this. The company's CEO, Arvind Krishna, acknowledged that AI had automated hundreds of roles in the HR department. But he also noted that the company's total headcount had grown, as talent was shifted into roles that required more "critical thinking."[94] The HR professionals whose careers were brittle were those whose value was based almost entirely on their proficiency in administrative processes (i.e., the very tasks that AI could easily handle). The HR professionals with resilient careers were those who had a more diversified skill set, including strategic talent management, organizational design, employee relations, and leadership development (i.e., the complex, human-centric skills that AI cannot replicate).

Ask yourself: is your professional identity tied to a single tool or a single, repeatable process? Are you the "Excel guru" whose primary value is your ability to build complex spreadsheets? Are you the graphic designer who has mastered one piece of software but has not developed skills in strategic branding or client communication? If so, your career model may be brittle. A resilient career is built on a portfolio of skills, with a strong foundation in the durable, human-centric competencies of the C.H.A.T. model.

The second warning sign of a brittle career is a lack of continuous learning. In a rapidly changing environment, the assumption that the skills that made you successful in the past will continue to do so in the future is a dangerous one. If you have not learned a significant new skill or taken on a challenging new type of project in the last few years, your career model may be brittle. The professionals who will thrive in the age of AI are those who have embraced the identity of a lifelong learner. They are constantly scanning the horizon for new trends, experimenting with new tools, and proactively upskilling to stay relevant.

Conclusion

In the new world of work, job security is not a passive state of being safe. It is an active process of being aware. The question "Is my job safe?" is rooted in an old, static model of careers. It implies that safety is an external condition that is granted to you. The better questions for the modern professional are: "Which parts of my job are most vulnerable to automation?" "How can I leverage AI to eliminate the drudgery from my work?" and "How can I reinvest that reclaimed time to double down on my uniquely human strengths?" These questions reframe you as the active agent in your own career story.

The Creep Risk Audit is your first, most important tool for answering these questions. It is a structured method for moving from a general sense of anxiety to a specific, actionable understanding of your personal risk profile. It provides the data you need to begin the process of intentional career evolution. By identifying your vulnerabilities and recognizing the warning signs of a brittle career model, you have taken the first and most important step toward building a future-proof professional life.

Now that you have audited the risks in your current role, it is time to build a proactive plan. The next chapter will provide a five-year upskilling roadmap to help you pivot without the panic.

Chapter 10: Pivot Without the Panic

Introduction

Amit Sharma was at a crossroads. His career in Quality Assurance (QA) was stable, but he could see the technological horizon shifting. The skills that had built his career were not the skills that would define the future. He saw the rise of artificial intelligence not as a distant threat, but as a present-day opportunity. Instead of waiting for disruption to happen to him, he decided to become the disruptor of his own career. He enrolled in an online program, the "Machine Learning Career Path Certification" from the platform AI Folks. For six months, he dedicated himself to learning a new and complex field, a process that required discipline and a clear sense of purpose. The pivot was a resounding success. "AI Folks helped me transition from a QA role to a Machine Learning Engineer in just six months," he reported.[95]

Sharma's story is a powerful testament to a new reality: reinvention is not just possible; it is becoming a necessary and achievable strategy for mid-career professionals. The results of your "Creep Risk" Audit in the last chapter may have been unsettling. Seeing the tasks that define your daily work categorized as "high potential for automation" can trigger a sense of panic. This panic is a specific and potent cocktail of fears: the fear of professional obsolescence, the fear that you are too old to learn a new skill, the fear that your years of experience have been rendered worthless, and the fear of being outmaneuvered by younger, more digitally native colleagues. It is the feeling that the ladder you have spent decades climbing is about to be kicked out from under you.

This chapter is the antidote to that panic. It is a practical guide to proactively reshaping your career through deliberate, strategic upskilling. Panic leads to paralysis or frantic, unfocused action. A plan, on the other hand, leads to progress. We will provide a template for a five-year roadmap that allows you to learn new skills without burning out, a structure designed to fit into the complex life of a working adult. We will then explore how to leverage your most valuable asset, your years of professional experience, as the foundation for your next chapter. This is not about starting over from scratch. It is about building on the wisdom you already possess to pivot with confidence and purpose.

Section 1: The 5-Year Upskilling Roadmap

The idea of "upskilling" can feel overwhelming. It conjures images of quitting your job to go back to school full-time, a prospect that is simply not realistic for most mid-career professionals with financial and family responsibilities. The key to a successful pivot is to reframe upskilling not as a massive, disruptive event, but as a manageable, long-term project. A five-year roadmap breaks down a daunting goal into a series of achievable steps, turning a vague aspiration into a concrete plan. It transforms anxiety into a series of focused, quarterly objectives.

Step 1: Define Your "North Star" (Years 1-2)

The first step in any journey is knowing your destination. Your "North Star" is the role or type of work you are aiming for in five years. This should be an informed decision, based on the principles we explored in Chapter 4. Look for roles that are resilient to automation: those that are human-centered, hybrid "AI + X" roles, or entirely new positions being created by the AI economy. Your goal is to move toward work that leverages your Human Edge, your creativity, humanity, adaptability, and critical thinking.

This initial phase is about research and exploration. Start by analyzing future-facing job descriptions. Go on LinkedIn and search for roles that seem interesting, but add modifiers like "AI," "automation," or "digital transformation." See what skills these roles require. What kind of language do they use? This will give you a clear picture of what the market is looking for. Next, conduct informational interviews. Find people who are already doing the kind of work you aspire to do and ask for fifteen minutes of their time. Ask them about their daily work, the skills they find most valuable, and the advice they would give to someone trying to enter the field.

A marketing manager, for example, might see that routine campaign analysis and content generation are being automated. His North Star might be to become a "Marketing Strategist Specializing in AI-Driven Personalization." This is a hybrid role that combines his existing marketing expertise with new skills in data analytics and AI ethics. He might arrive at this North Star after noticing that the job descriptions for senior marketing roles at his dream companies increasingly mention skills like "customer data platforms," "personalization at scale," and "ethical data use."

Before fully committing to a North Star, it is wise to engage in a bit of "career prototyping." This means running small, low-cost experiments to test your interest and aptitude for a new field. If you are considering a pivot to data analytics, do not immediately enroll in an expensive, year-long program. Start by taking a single, introductory online course. Spend a weekend working through a free tutorial. Does the work genuinely interest you? Do you enjoy the process of finding stories in the data? These small experiments can save you a significant amount of time and money, and they can help you refine your North Star based on real-world experience rather than just speculation.

Step 2: Deconstruct the Goal and Choose Your Learning Modality (Year 2)

Once you have a North Star, you need to deconstruct it into a set of specific, learnable skills. What are the concrete competencies required for that role? Our aspiring Marketing Strategist would need to add skills like "Data Analytics," "Project Management," and "AI Ethics" to his existing marketing toolkit. This deconstruction turns a big, intimidating goal into a checklist of manageable learning objectives.

With this list of skills, you can now choose the right learning modality for your life and budget. The modern educational landscape offers a wide array of options designed for busy professionals.

- **Professional Certificates:** Platforms like Coursera and Google offer professional certificate programs that are designed to be completed part-time over several months. These are often created in partnership with industry leaders and are focused on teaching job-ready skills. The data shows these are highly effective. Coursera notes that 72 percent of employers say they are more likely to hire a candidate with a professional certificate, and enrollments in these programs have surged in recent years.[96] These are an excellent choice for acquiring a specific, in-demand skill in a structured and efficient way.

- **University-Backed Online Courses**: Platforms like edX offer courses and "MicroMasters" programs from top universities like MIT and Harvard. These can provide a more rigorous, academically grounded approach to a new subject, offering a university credential without the time and expense of a full degree program.

- **Bootcamps**: For those looking for a more intensive, immersive experience, a part-time coding or data science bootcamp can be a powerful option. These programs are designed for career switchers and have a strong focus on building a portfolio of projects. Many now offer flexible, evening, and weekend schedules to accommodate working professionals.

- **Self-Directed Learning:** For the highly motivated, a self-directed path using free resources from platforms like Microsoft Learn, combined with a subscription to a platform like LinkedIn Learning, can be a cost-effective option. LinkedIn's data shows that employees who set clear career goals engage in four times more learning on their platform, suggesting that a self-directed approach is most effective when it is part of a structured plan.[97]

The story of one marketing manager provides a perfect example of this process in action. While between jobs, he identified a skills gap and completed two Google Career Certificates: one in Data Analytics and one in Project Management. This targeted upskilling had a direct and immediate impact on his career. "I probably use each equally in my new role," he reported. He was about to receive a promotion that "would not have been possible without the certifications."[98] He did not go back for a full degree. He identified the specific skills he needed and chose a learning modality that was efficient, affordable, and directly relevant to his career goals.

Step 3: Build Your Proof of Work (Years 3-4)

As you acquire new skills, you must immediately put them into practice. This is the project-building phase of your roadmap. As we discussed in Chapter 7, proof of work is the ultimate differentiator. For a mid-career professional, this does not have to mean building a public side project. Your current job can be the perfect laboratory for your new skills. Volunteer to lead the pilot program for a new AI tool. Offer to create a new, automated report for your team and document the process. Find a small, inefficient workflow in your department and use your new project management skills to redesign it.

Proposing these internal projects requires a degree of political savvy. You must frame your initiative not as a personal learning exercise, but as a direct benefit to the team and the company. You might approach your manager and say, "I've been learning about AI-powered data analysis, and I have an idea for how we could automate the weekly sales report. I believe this could save our team about five hours a week, freeing us up to focus on more strategic client outreach. I'd like to volunteer to spend a few hours building a prototype to see if it's feasible." This approach demonstrates initiative, a focus on business value, and a collaborative spirit. These internal projects are powerful forms of proof of work that demonstrate your initiative and your ability to apply new skills to create real business value.

Step 4: Signal Your Pivot (Year 5)

The final year of your roadmap is about signaling your new identity to the professional world. This is when you begin to actively seek out opportunities in your target role, either within your current company or at a new one. Your proof of work is now your primary marketing tool. You will update your LinkedIn profile to reflect your new skills, adding your certificates and linking to your portfolio projects. You will use the "portfolio stacking" techniques from the previous chapter, perhaps writing a blog post about what you learned from your data analytics project or sharing your white paper on AI ethics with your network. You will start to change the way you talk about yourself in meetings and performance reviews, framing your contributions in the language of your new, desired role. This five-year structure turns a daunting pivot into a series of manageable steps. It is a marathon, not a sprint, a process of gradual but deliberate transformation that respects the realities of a mid-career professional's life.

Section 2: Translating Experience into Leverage

For many mid-career professionals, one of the biggest sources of anxiety is the fear that their years of experience have become a liability, a set of obsolete skills in a rapidly changing world. This fear is not only unfounded; it is the exact opposite of the truth. In the age of AI, your experience is not a liability; it is your most valuable asset. The key is to learn how to translate that experience into leverage.

The reason experience is becoming more valuable is that as AI handles more of the routine, analytical tasks, the skills that are left, the skills that differentiate human professionals, are precisely the ones that can only be developed through years of real-world experience. A recent report from ManpowerGroup found that a third of employers believe that skills like ethical judgment, customer empathy, team management, and strategic thinking cannot be replaced by AI.[99] An HR industry report echoed this, with 83 percent of leaders agreeing that AI will make these human skills even more vital.[100] The data is clear: the market is placing an ever-higher premium on the durable, human-centric competencies of the C.H.A.T. model.

Patrick Smith, a technology executive at the software company Certara, explained why this is the case. "Effective use of AI requires someone with the experience and critical thinking skills to understand the model's insights in the context of a wider industry," he stated. "For example, when using generative AI to draft documents, such as regulatory submissions for the pharmaceutical industry, one must be able to contextualize the information to ensure the output's consistency, accuracy and compliance."[101]

This is a profoundly important insight. An AI is a powerful engine, but it lacks context. It is a tool without wisdom. We can think of this as the difference between the "knowledge layer" and the "wisdom layer." An AI operates at the knowledge layer. It can access and process vast amounts of information. But an experienced professional operates at the wisdom layer. They provide the context that the machine lacks. They know the history of the project, the personalities of the key stakeholders, the unwritten rules of the company culture, and the subtle dynamics of the market. This contextual intelligence is a form of expertise that can only be built over time, and it is the key to unlocking the true value of AI.

The strategic challenge for a mid-career professional is to learn how to rebrand their experience in this new context. You must learn to articulate your value not in terms of the tasks you perform, but in terms of the human-centric skills you possess. For example:

- A customer support manager is not just "managing a team of reps." They are "leading a team in complex, high-stakes conflict resolution and de-escalation, and mentoring junior employees in the art of building long-term customer relationships."
- A financial analyst is not just "building financial models." They are "applying critical judgment to ambiguous financial data, communicating complex insights to non-technical stakeholders, and acting as a trusted advisor to leadership on strategic decisions."
- A project manager is not just "managing timelines and budgets." They are "facilitating collaboration across diverse, cross-functional teams, navigating complex organizational politics, and adapting to unexpected challenges to ensure project success."

Notice how this reframing shifts the focus from the automatable tasks to the durable human skills. This is how you translate your experience into leverage. You must audit your own career history through the lens of the C.H.A.T. model and learn to tell a story about your work that highlights your creativity, your humanity, your adaptability, and your critical thinking.

Conclusion

The prospect of a mid-career pivot in the age of AI can feel like a daunting climb up a steep mountain. But it is a climb that you are uniquely equipped to make. The panic that often accompanies the thought of professional reinvention can be replaced by a sense of purpose and control when you have a clear plan. The five-year upskilling roadmap provides that plan. It is a structured, manageable approach to acquiring the new skills you need without upending your life. It is a strategy for building your future self, one step at a time.

But new skills alone are not enough. The true power of a mid-career pivot lies in the fusion of the new with the old. Your years of experience are not a weight holding you back; they are the foundation upon which you will build your next chapter. Your deep industry knowledge, your nuanced understanding of human nature, and your hard-won wisdom are the very assets that are becoming more valuable in a world of intelligent machines. By learning to reframe and articulate this value, you position yourself not as a victim of change, but as a sought-after expert who can provide the human context that AI will always lack.

Now that you have a plan to acquire new skills and a strategy to leverage your existing wisdom, it is time to fuse them together. The next chapter will show you how to create the ultimate professional hybrid: Human + Machine.

Chapter 11: Human + Machine = You 2.0

Introduction

For a senior auditor at a large consulting firm, the end of every quarter brought a familiar sense of dread. The task was always the same: to produce a series of detailed internal audit reports for a major client. The process was a painstaking, manual grind. The "before" picture was a study in professional drudgery. It began with days spent gathering data from a dozen different, disconnected systems: spreadsheets from finance, logs from IT, reports from operations. Then came the tedious work of reconciliation, manually cross-referencing thousands of lines of data to spot inconsistencies. Finally, there was the writing itself, a repetitive process of filling out a standardized template, describing findings, and documenting evidence. The entire cycle for a single report consumed the better part of a week, a significant block of time spent on low-value, mechanical work that left little room for deep, strategic thinking.

The "after" picture looks radically different. The firm implemented an AI assistant, a tool similar to Microsoft Copilot, integrated directly into their workflow. Now, the auditor starts not by gathering data, but by giving the AI a prompt: "Generate a preliminary internal audit report for Q3 for Client X, using data from the finance, IT, and operations dashboards. Highlight any anomalies that exceed a 5 percent variance from the previous quarter." The AI executes the drudgery. It accesses the disparate systems, synthesizes the data, populates the report template, and flags the most significant outliers for human review. The result, according to a case study of a business that implemented such a tool, was a 30 percent reduction in the time required to write these reports.[102]

This is not a story about a person being replaced. It is a story about a professional being amplified. The auditor's week of tedious labor has been compressed into a day or two of focused, high-value work. She now spends her time not on data entry, but on investigating the anomalies the AI has surfaced, applying her years of experience and critical judgment to understand the why behind the numbers, and advising her client on strategic improvements. She has been transformed from a diligent producer of reports into a trusted strategic advisor. This is the promise of the human-machine partnership. It is the upgrade to You 2.0, a version of your professional self that is faster, more insightful, and more valuable than ever before. This chapter will show you how to achieve this upgrade. We will explore how AI acts as a force multiplier for your existing skills and how you can begin to reimagine your role in a world of augmented insight.

Section 1: AI as a Force Multiplier

The true power of artificial intelligence in the workplace is not that it possesses a superhuman intelligence, but that it offers a form of superhuman leverage. It is a force multiplier, a tool that can take your existing skills, knowledge, and expertise and amplify their impact by an order of magnitude. For the mid-career professional, this is a profound opportunity. You do not need to learn an entirely new profession. You need to learn how to apply this new source of leverage to the profession you have already mastered. This is happening right now across every major non-technical field, as professionals learn to partner with

AI to automate their drudgery and supercharge their most valuable human skills.

In the world of finance and accounting, the core work has always been a blend of meticulous, rule-based tasks and high-level strategic judgment. For decades, the former has consumed the majority of the time. An accountant's day could be filled with what one analysis calls "tedious financial activities such as data entry, reconciliation and report generation."[103] This is the work of making sure the numbers are correct and in the right place. It is vital, but it is not where the greatest value is created. An AI assistant like Microsoft Copilot fundamentally inverts this equation. It excels at rule-based, repetitive work. It can automate the process of pulling data from bank statements and invoices, perform reconciliations in seconds that would take a human hours, and generate the first drafts of standard financial reports.

This automation frees the human accountant or financial analyst to operate at a higher level. Instead of spending their time on the drudgery of data validation, they can focus on the more complex and valuable work of forecasting, scenario modeling, and strategic analysis. They can spend less time answering the question, "What were our revenues last quarter?" and more time exploring the question, "What are the three most likely scenarios for our revenue next year, and what are the key drivers we should be watching?"

The AI handles the mechanical processing of historical data, allowing the human to focus on the forward-looking application of judgment and wisdom. This transforms the finance professional from a historian of the company's past to an architect of its future. A 2025 case study of a business using these tools found that this partnership resulted in a productivity increase of 10 to 20 percent for 84 percent of the employees using the AI, saving a total of more than 2,300 person-hours that could be reinvested in more strategic work.[104]

In marketing, the same dynamic is at play. A marketing manager's job is a constant balancing act between creative ideation and data-driven analysis. Both are time-consuming. An AI assistant can act as a force multiplier on both fronts. On the analytical side, it can sift through vast amounts of campaign data to identify which customer segments are responding best to a particular message or which channels are providing the highest return on investment. This allows the marketing team to make faster, more data-informed decisions about where to allocate their budget and effort.

On the creative side, AI acts as a tireless brainstorming partner. It can "auto-generate targeted email copy or SEO briefs," which "enables marketing teams to create more personalized campaigns" with higher engagement.[105] The human marketer's role in this new workflow shifts from being a sole creator to being a creative director. They provide the strategic brief, the core insight into the customer's emotional needs, and the understanding of the brand's voice. The AI then generates a dozen different versions of an email subject line or a social media post. The marketer's job is to curate, to select the best option, and to refine it with a human touch. This partnership allows a small team to achieve a level of personalization and testing that was previously only possible for the largest, best-resourced corporations. It multiplies their creative output, allowing them to run more experiments and learn more quickly what resonates with their audience.

In the field of sales, one of the most persistent complaints from sales professionals is the amount of time they are forced to spend on administrative tasks instead of actually selling. A significant portion of their week can be consumed by updating the CRM system, logging calls, tracking leads, and writing follow-up emails. This is all time spent away from the core, value-creating activity of building relationships with customers.

An AI assistant integrated into the sales workflow can automate much of this administrative burden. It can summarize call recordings and automatically update the CRM with key details. It can track a lead's activity and prompt the salesperson when it is the optimal time to follow up. It can even suggest personalized pitches by analyzing a prospect's LinkedIn profile and company news. This frees the sales representative to spend the majority of their time on the uniquely human aspects of their job: building rapport, understanding a customer's deep-seated needs, navigating complex negotiations, and closing deals.[106] The AI handles the logistics of the sales process, allowing the human to focus on the psychology of it.

Across all these fields, the pattern is the same. The AI is not replacing the expert. It is augmenting them, acting as a force multiplier that dramatically increases their speed, accuracy, and creative capacity. It automates drudgery to amplify meaningful work. The sentiment of a customer support manager in a recent survey captures this new reality perfectly: "AI has made my job easier because now I have a tool that can assist anytime and provide suggestions immediately."[107] This is the essence of the You 2.0 upgrade. It is about partnering with a tool that is always on, always ready to assist, and capable of handling the repetitive work, freeing you to bring your best and most human self to your most important challenges.

Section 2: Reimagining Your Role with Augmented Insight

The arrival of a powerful AI assistant does not just make you faster at your old job; it gives you the opportunity to create a new and better one. The most profound shift for the mid-career professional is the move from being an executor of tasks to being a director of systems. Your value is no longer measured by the speed at which you can complete a process, but by the wisdom with which you can design and oversee it. This is not a demotion to a passive, button-pushing role. It is a promotion to a more strategic, human-centric position where your experience and judgment become more valuable than ever before.

This transformation is already underway, as forward-thinking companies are actively redesigning roles to place humans in a position of oversight, not drudgery. At IBM, the HR group that automated routine recruiting tasks did not simply shrink. Instead, its employees were freed to become strategic partners to the business. The time they once spent manually screening resumes and scheduling interviews is now spent on higher-level challenges like analyzing workforce trends, designing new career development programs, and advising senior leaders on talent strategy and corporate culture.[108] They have moved from the transactional to the transformational.

The IKEA model provides another powerful blueprint for this shift. The employees who once answered a constant stream of repetitive phone calls are being retrained as interior design advisors. The AI chatbot handles the basic queries, freeing the human employees to engage in creative, collaborative problem-solving with customers.[109] This is a classic example of moving human capital up the value chain. The company recognized that the people answering the phones possessed deep product knowledge and valuable customer interaction skills. Instead of discarding that talent, they chose to elevate it, transforming a cost center into a new source of revenue and customer delight.

This pattern is not limited to a few innovative companies; it is an industry-wide trend. A 2025 Gallup report highlights the banking industry as a prime example of this role redesign in action. For decades, the work of a loan officer was heavily weighted toward the administrative drudgery of processing paperwork. Today, AI is increasingly handling the repetitive, data-heavy tasks associated with loan applications. This automation has redesigned the role of the human banker. They are now freed from the back office to spend more time in the front office, focusing on the high-value, uniquely human work of advising clients, understanding their complex financial situations, and building the long-term, trust-based relationships that are the bedrock of the banking business.[110] The AI handles the paperwork; the human handles the partnership.

Even in the world of agile project management, this shift is visible. A scrum master's role is to facilitate the team's process, a job that has traditionally involved a great deal of administrative work, such as taking detailed notes during meetings and manually tracking action items. New AI tools can now transcribe meetings in real time and automatically generate summaries and lists of tasks. This frees the scrum master to focus on their most important and most human function: observing team dynamics, coaching members through interpersonal challenges, and removing the human-centered roadblocks that are the true impediments to progress.[111]

What all these examples have in common is a fundamental redefinition of professional value. The mid-career worker of the past was often valued for their efficiency and their deep knowledge of established processes. The mid-career professional of the future will be valued for their ability to supervise, to curate, and to apply strategic judgment to the output of intelligent systems. Your role is to be the human-in-the-loop, the wisdom layer on top of the AI's knowledge layer.

This new model of work aligns perfectly with what professionals themselves desire. The Stanford HAI study on worker preferences introduced a "Human Agency Scale" to measure the ideal level of collaboration between humans and AI. The study found that for most tasks, workers do not want full automation, nor do they want to be relegated to the role of a simple assistant who just follows the AI's orders. The most desired level of collaboration, the one that workers found most productive and satisfying, was "Equal Partnership."[112] This is a state where the human and the AI work together as a team, with each contributing their unique strengths to achieve a result that is superior to what either could accomplish alone.

This is the goal you should be aiming for as you reimagine your role. You are not a servant to the AI, nor is it your servant. You are collaborators. You provide the strategy, the context, the ethical oversight, and the critical judgment. The AI provides the speed, the data processing power, and the tireless execution of routine tasks. You are the architect; the AI is the master builder. You are the editor-in-chief; the AI is the brilliant but sometimes unreliable staff writer. This is the definition of augmented insight. It is a partnership that keeps you in control, making you the orchestrator of the technology, not a victim of it.

Conclusion

The formula for professional success in the age of AI is no longer just about individual skill; it is about the synergy you can create between your own expertise and the capabilities of the machine. The equation is simple but profound: Human + Machine = You 2.0. This is not a distant, futuristic concept. As we have seen, mid-career professionals across every industry are already living this reality, using AI as a powerful force multiplier to automate their drudgery, amplify their creativity, and deliver unprecedented value.

The key takeaway from this chapter is that AI is a powerful amplifier for human expertise. It takes the knowledge and wisdom you have accumulated over your career and gives it a new and more powerful voice. The combination of your years of experience, the "wisdom layer", with the AI's speed and knowledge creates an exponential increase in your professional impact. This is the definitive path to becoming indispensable in the new world of work. By embracing this partnership, you are not just protecting your career from the threat of automation; you are actively redesigning it to be more strategic, more creative, and more fulfilling. The drudgery that may have led to burnout can now be delegated to your machine colleague, freeing you to focus on the complex, collaborative, and deeply human challenges that are the most engaging parts of any profession. This is your chance to fall in love with your career again by redesigning it around what you do best.

Understanding this new partnership model is the first step. Mastering the practical skills to make it a reality is the next. Now that you understand the "what" and the "why" of the human-machine partnership, the next chapter will provide the "how." It is your tactical playbook for becoming a true AI power user at work, giving you the specific techniques to build the automated workflows and augmented systems that will define your new role as You 2.0.

Chapter 12: Becoming an AI Power User at Work

Introduction

At the airline Virgin Atlantic, a quiet revolution is taking place, led not by data scientists or software engineers, but by employees from Flight Operations, Finance, and the People Team. In March 2025, the company launched an "AI Champion" apprenticeship, a 13-month program designed to empower staff from non-technical departments to lead the adoption of artificial intelligence. These employees are learning the fundamentals of AI, automation, and prompt engineering, not to change their careers, but to transform them. They are being trained to become internal advocates, the go-to experts who can spot opportunities for innovation within their own departments and guide their colleagues in using these new tools effectively and responsibly.[113]

This initiative is a powerful illustration of a new career archetype emerging in the modern workplace: the non-technical AI power user. This is the mid-career professional who, through curiosity and initiative, becomes the indispensable bridge between the technology's potential and the practical, day-to-day work of their team. They are not just users of AI; they are orchestrators of it. They do not just complete their tasks more efficiently; they fundamentally redesign how the work gets done. The previous chapter showed you how to partner with AI to become You 2.0. This chapter provides the advanced playbook for making that partnership a source of influence and impact. We will explore how to build your own custom automation engines without writing a single line of code and how to run focused experiments to discover new ways to improve your team's processes. This is how you move from personal productivity to team-wide amplification.

Section 1: Building Your Own Automation Engine

The leap from a proficient user to a power user happens when you stop performing repetitive tasks and start building systems to perform them for you. This is the mindset of the automator. It is the ability to look at a workflow, deconstruct it into its component parts, and identify the manual, repetitive steps that can be handed over to a machine. In the past, this kind of system-building was the exclusive domain of software developers. Today, the rise of powerful and intuitive no-code platforms has democratized this capability, giving any motivated professional the ability to build their own custom automation engines.

The leaders in this space are platforms like Zapier and Make.com. These tools act as a universal translator for the internet, allowing you to connect thousands of different web applications and create automated workflows that pass information between them. The logic is simple and intuitive, based on the concept of "triggers" and "actions." A trigger is an event that starts the workflow (e.g., "when a new email arrives in my inbox with the word 'invoice' in the subject line"). An action is the task that is performed in response (e.g., "save the attachment from that email to a specific folder in Google Drive and send me a notification in Slack"). By chaining these simple triggers and actions together, you can build surprisingly sophisticated automations.

142

The true power of these platforms in the modern era is their deep integration with artificial intelligence. You can now insert an AI, like the model that powers ChatGPT, as a step in any workflow. This allows you to add a layer of intelligence to your automations, moving beyond simple data transfer to complex data analysis and generation. The team at Zapier calls this "embedding AI into your workflows." Instead of constantly switching between your work applications and a separate AI tool, you can build a system where the AI is a seamless, invisible part of the process.[114]

Let's explore a few practical examples of how a mid-career professional could use this to solve real business problems.

- **Automating Email Triage for a Sales Team**: A sales operations manager notices that her team is spending hours each day sifting through a generic "sales@company.com" inbox to find the high-priority leads. She could build a simple automation engine to solve this. The workflow might look like this:
  1. **Trigger**: When a new email arrives in the sales inbox.
  2. **Action 1 (AI Analysis)**: Send the body of the email to an AI with a prompt: "Analyze this sales inquiry. Based on the sender's title, company size, and the specific questions they are asking, classify this lead as 'High Priority,' 'Medium Priority,' or 'Low Priority.' Also, summarize the inquiry into a single sentence."
  3. **Action 2 (Routing)**: Based on the AI's classification, automatically forward the email to the appropriate person or team. High-priority leads

could be sent directly to the senior sales executives, while low-priority inquiries could be routed to a junior team member or sent an automated response.

4. **Action 3 (Notification)**: Post the AI's one-sentence summary to a dedicated Slack channel, giving the entire team real-time visibility into the sales pipeline.

This simple engine, built with no code, transforms a chaotic, manual process into an intelligent, automated system. It saves the team hours of administrative drudgery and ensures that the most valuable leads are acted upon immediately.

- **Automating Content Creation for a Marketing Team**: A content marketing manager is responsible for repurposing the company's long-form blog posts into a variety of social media assets. This is a time-consuming, manual process. She could build an automation engine to handle the first draft of this work.

  1. **Trigger**: When a new blog post is published on the company's website.

  2. **Action 1 (AI Repurposing)**: Send the text of the blog post to an AI with a series of prompts: "Generate three different, engaging headlines for this blog post suitable for LinkedIn," "Write a 280-character summary of this post suitable for X (formerly Twitter)," and "Create a five-point bulleted list of the key takeaways from this article."

  3. **Action 2 (Draft Creation)**: Take the AI-generated content and automatically create a

new draft document in a shared Google Drive, complete with the different social media options.

4. **Action 3 (Notification)**: Notify the social media manager in their project management tool (like Asana or Trello) that a new set of social media drafts is ready for their review and refinement.

This workflow does not replace the social media manager. It empowers them. It handles the initial, repetitive work of summarizing and reformatting, allowing the human expert to focus on the higher-value tasks of refining the copy, selecting the right visuals, and engaging with the audience.

Building these kinds of automation engines is a powerful way to create leverage. It allows you to solve problems not just for yourself, but for your entire team. The professional who can identify a bottleneck in a business process and then design and build an automated solution becomes an invaluable asset. They are no longer just a participant in the workflow; they are the architect of a more efficient and intelligent way of working.

Section 2: Running Prompt Sprints and Experiments

Becoming a power user is not just about building static automations; it is also about fostering a dynamic culture of experimentation. One of the most effective ways to do this is by running "prompt sprints." A prompt sprint is a short, focused, collaborative experiment designed to discover how AI can be used to improve a specific team process or solve a particular business problem. It is a way to move AI usage out of the shadows and into the open, turning it from a solo activity into a team sport.

The concept is inspired by the "design sprints" used in the software development world, but it is adapted for a non-technical audience. The goal is to create a low-stakes, time-boxed environment where team members can come together to brainstorm, test, and refine prompts for a specific use case. This approach is a powerful antidote to the fear and uncertainty that often surrounds the introduction of new AI tools. It is an active, hands-on process that demystifies the technology and empowers employees to become co-creators of their own augmented workflows.

A real-world example of this in action comes from NYU Langone Health. In 2023, the organization held an AI "Prompt-a-Thon," a large-scale prompt sprint designed to find AI-powered solutions for real-world healthcare challenges. The event brought together diverse teams of clinicians, educators, and researchers to experiment with generative AI using de-identified patient data. The goal was to move beyond abstract discussions and empower the workforce to explore practical applications. Teams collaborated to develop and refine prompts for specific business processes, such as improving patient education materials, streamlining the process of summarizing scientific literature for grant applications, and even reviewing clinical notes to flag potential drug interactions. The event was an overwhelming success, with participants reporting a significant increase in their confidence and a greater likelihood of integrating AI into their daily work.[115]

While a large-scale "Prompt-a-Thon" might be ambitious, you can apply the core principles of the prompt sprint on a much smaller scale within your own team. Here is a simple, four-step framework for running your first sprint:

Step 1: Identify a High-Friction, Low-Value Task

The best candidate for a prompt sprint is a task that everyone on the team dislikes and that consumes a disproportionate amount of time for the value it creates. This could be the process of writing weekly status reports, summarizing customer feedback, or brainstorming initial ideas for a new project. The key is to choose a problem that is widely recognized as a pain point.

Step 2: Assemble a Small Group and Time-Box the Experiment

You do not need the whole department. A small group of three to five motivated colleagues is ideal. Schedule a single, 90-minute meeting. The time constraint is important; it creates a sense of urgency and focuses the energy on rapid experimentation rather than endless debate.

Step 3: Brainstorm and Test Prompts Collaboratively

In the first part of the meeting, have everyone brainstorm different ways to phrase a prompt to solve the target problem. For example, if the problem is writing weekly status reports, the prompts might range from a simple "Summarize the following project updates into a one-page report" to a more sophisticated, persona-driven prompt like "Act as a senior project manager. I will provide you with a list of updates from my team members. Your task is to synthesize these updates into a concise, professional status report. The report should have three sections: Key Accomplishments This Week, Challenges and Roadblocks, and Priorities for Next Week. The tone should be confident and clear." In the second part of the meeting, have the team test these different prompts in real time, using actual project data.

Compare the outputs. Which prompt produced the most useful result? Which one was the most accurate?

Step 4: Refine and Share the Winning Prompt

Based on the results of your experiment, work together to refine the best-performing prompt into a "golden prompt" that the whole team can use. Document this prompt and share it in a team-wide channel, along with a brief explanation of how to use it. By doing this, you are not just solving a problem; you are creating a reusable asset that increases the collective intelligence of your team.

Running these kinds of small, regular experiments has a powerful cultural impact. It fosters a mindset of continuous improvement and collaborative problem-solving. It builds psychological safety around the use of AI, signaling that it is a tool for everyone to experiment with, not a secret weapon for a select few. And it positions you, the organizer of the sprint, as a proactive leader and an innovator, regardless of your official job title.

Section 3: Using AI to Amplify Team Intelligence

The ultimate goal of becoming an AI power user at work is to move beyond personal productivity and begin to amplify the intelligence and effectiveness of your entire team. This is the highest level of leverage, where your skills create a ripple effect that benefits everyone around you. This is not about showing off your technical prowess; it is about being a generous and effective collaborator who uses AI to make the team smarter, more aligned, and more creative. There are several practical ways to do this.

First, you can use AI to solve the persistent problem of information asymmetry in any collaborative project. In any team, knowledge is often siloed. The engineering team has deep technical knowledge, the marketing team has insights into the customer, and the sales team understands the competitive landscape. The success of a project often depends on how well this distributed knowledge can be shared and synthesized. An AI can act as a powerful information hub, breaking down these silos.

Imagine your team has just concluded a two-hour project kickoff meeting, with representatives from five different departments. The conversation was wide-ranging and complex. As a power user, you can take the AI-generated transcript of that meeting and use a series of prompts to create a suite of customized assets for the team. For the executive sponsor, you could generate a one-paragraph executive summary that highlights the key decisions made and the project's primary business goals. For the project manager, you could generate a detailed list of all the action items, complete with assigned owners and deadlines. For the technical lead, you could extract all the specific discussions related to technical requirements and potential roadblocks. By creating these tailored summaries, you ensure that everyone on the team has a clear and shared understanding of the project, regardless of their individual perspective. This simple act of AI-powered synthesis can prevent countless misunderstandings and misalignments down the road.

Second, you can use AI to facilitate more effective and creative brainstorming sessions. Traditional brainstorming can often be dominated by the loudest voices in the room, and it can be difficult to move beyond the first few obvious ideas. An AI can be used to structure and supercharge this process. Before a brainstorming meeting, you could ask an AI to "act as a world-class innovation consultant and generate 20 unconventional ideas for how a sustainable coffee brand could market itself to a Gen Z audience." You can then bring this list of AI-generated ideas to the meeting as a starting point. This immediately elevates the conversation, moving the team beyond the blank page and providing a diverse set of initial concepts to react to and build upon.

During the meeting, you can use the AI in real time to explore and expand on the team's ideas. If a team member suggests a new product idea, you could ask the AI to "instantly generate a press release for this new product" or "write a short script for a 30-second video ad." Seeing an idea instantly brought to life in this way can be a powerful catalyst for further creative thinking. This is a form of collaborative ideation where the AI acts as a tireless and infinitely creative junior team member, allowing the human team to operate at a higher, more strategic level.

Finally, becoming the team's go-to AI expert is a powerful form of informal leadership. As your colleagues see you using AI to solve problems and improve processes, they will naturally start to come to you for advice. You can formalize this by hosting informal "AI office hours" or a monthly lunch-and-learn where you share a new tool or a useful prompting technique you have discovered. This does not require you to be a technical genius. It just requires you to be one step ahead of your colleagues and generous with your knowledge.

This practice of sharing your expertise has a dual benefit. It obviously helps your colleagues become more effective, increasing the overall productivity of the team. But it also has a profound impact on your own career. By becoming the person who helps others navigate this new technological landscape, you build a reputation as a leader, an innovator, and a valuable team player. This is the kind of social capital that leads to new opportunities, greater influence, and a more resilient and indispensable role within your organization. The data supports this; a recent LinkedIn survey found that 75 percent of workers are already using AI at work, often without any formal company policy.[116] By being the person who brings this "shadow AI" usage out into the open and provides guidance and support, you are meeting a real and urgent need.

Conclusion

Becoming an AI power user at work is about a fundamental shift in mindset. It is a move from being a passive recipient of tasks to being a proactive designer of systems. It is about seeing AI not as a threat to your job, but as the most powerful tool you have ever been given to redesign it for the better. This is not a journey that requires a technical background or a formal title. It is a path that is open to any mid-career professional with a healthy dose of curiosity and a willingness to experiment.

The playbook we have outlined in this chapter provides a clear, step-by-step guide to making this transition. By learning to build your own automation engines with no-code tools, you can eliminate the drudgery from your work and the work of your team, freeing up human talent for higher-value challenges. By running prompt sprints and other collaborative experiments, you can demystify the technology and foster a culture of innovation and continuous improvement. And by using AI to amplify the collective intelligence of your team, you can move beyond personal productivity to create a wider and more lasting impact.

The common thread that runs through all these practices is a proactive, generous, and strategic approach to technology. The power user is not just trying to make their own life easier; they are constantly looking for opportunities to use AI to solve problems, create value, and elevate the performance of the entire team. This mindset is the key to transforming your professional identity. You are no longer just a marketing manager, a financial analyst, or a project coordinator. You are an AI-augmented professional, an innovator, and a leader. This new influence, this new reputation as the go-to AI expert on your team, creates a natural and powerful path to formal leadership. The next chapter will explore how to walk that path, providing a guide to the new skills and responsibilities of leading in the age of AI.

Chapter 13: Leading in the Age of AI

Introduction

Imagine you are a manager, and you have just been given access to a powerful new AI tool that promises to revolutionize your team's productivity. You are genuinely excited. You see its potential to automate the tedious reports that consume your team's Monday mornings, to analyze customer data in seconds, and to free everyone up for more creative, strategic work. You call a team meeting, and with great enthusiasm, you announce the rollout of this new technology. You expect applause, or at least a sense of optimistic curiosity. Instead, you are met with a wall of anxious silence. Your team members are not looking at the screen; they are looking at each other. Their faces betray a single, unspoken question: Is this the tool that is going to replace me?

This is the central dilemma for the modern leader. In an age of profound technological disruption, your greatest challenge is not implementing the technology; it is managing the human response to it. The introduction of AI into a team is not like the introduction of a new email client or a new spreadsheet program. Those were tools that changed the mechanics of communication and calculation. AI is a tool that touches the mechanics of cognition itself. It operates in the realm of tasks (e.g., writing, analyzing, creating) that were once the exclusive domain of the human knowledge worker. This makes its arrival a deeply personal and often threatening event for the people on your team.

The skills that made you a successful manager in the past, your ability to manage projects, allocate resources, and enforce processes, are still necessary, but they are no longer sufficient. The new, defining competency of leadership is the ability to guide a team through a period of deep uncertainty with empathy, transparency, and a clear, human-centered vision. This chapter is a playbook for that new form of leadership. We will explore how to manage augmented teams by putting people first, and we will redefine the leader's role as a vital bridge between the power of technology and the potential of your people.

Section 1: Managing Augmented Teams with Empathy

The temptation for many organizations is to treat the rollout of a new AI tool as a simple IT project. They focus on the technical implementation, the training modules, and the productivity metrics. But this approach completely misses the most important part of the equation: the emotional and psychological impact on the employees who are being asked to change the way they work. A successful AI adoption is not a technology project; it is a change management project, and the most effective change management is rooted in empathy.

The data on this is stark. A 2024 study from Workday revealed a significant "empathy gap" in the workplace. While 82 percent of employees said that human connection will be more important in the age of AI, only 65 percent of managers agreed.[117] This gap is a breeding ground for the kind of fear and resistance that can doom any new initiative. When a leader announces a new AI tool, an employee's internal monologue is often a rapid-fire sequence of anxieties. Does my boss think a machine can do my job better than me? Is this the first step toward eliminating my role? Will I be able to learn this new technology fast enough? Will I be monitored more closely? Will this take away the parts of my job I actually enjoy? Your team does not just need to know how to use the new tool; they need to feel understood, supported, and valued throughout the transition. Empathetic leadership in this context is not about being "soft"; it is about being smart. It is about recognizing that your team's psychological safety is a prerequisite for their engagement and innovation.

A powerful case study in this human-centered approach comes from the global professional services firm KPMG. When the company decided to roll out a firm-wide generative AI tool, it deliberately chose a path of collaboration over a top-down mandate. The firm partnered with Microsoft to create "KymChat," a secure, internal version of ChatGPT. This first step was itself an act of empathy. By creating a private, sandboxed environment, KPMG provided a safe space for employees to experiment without the fear of exposing confidential client data or breaking a critical system. It signaled to the workforce that this was a tool for learning and exploration, not just for production.[118]

Crucially, KPMG invested heavily in employee education and involvement. They did not just send out a memo with a link to the new tool. They launched the "Eclipse AI Academy" and hosted "24 hours of AI" events, global, interactive sessions designed to upskill staff and build confidence in a collaborative and even celebratory environment. This approach framed AI not as a threat to be managed, but as an opportunity to be explored together. The results were a testament to this human-centric strategy. Nearly all employees participated in the experimental programs, and KymChat processed over 1.7 million prompts from 13,000 unique users in its initial phase, demonstrating widespread, voluntary adoption. KPMG succeeded because it treated its employees as partners in the transformation, not as targets of it.

This empathetic approach can be broken down into a few key practices for any leader to follow. First, as KPMG demonstrated, you must involve, not impose. Before you roll out a new tool, form a small working group of influential members from your team to act as an advisory board. This group should include not just your most tech-savvy employees, but also your most respected skeptics. Give them early access to the technology and empower them to help you co-create the implementation plan. This turns potential skeptics into advocates and ensures that the rollout is designed to solve the team's real-world problems, not just to meet a top-down corporate objective.

Second, you must communicate the "why," not just the "what." Your team needs to understand the strategic rationale behind the change. Is the goal to improve the customer experience? To free up time for more creative work? To stay ahead of the competition? A clear and compelling "why" provides a sense of shared purpose. Research from Gallup and Workday reinforces this, noting that "workplace policies are no replacement for a direct manager who understands the individual and the situation."[119] This means having direct, honest conversations. Acknowledge the team's anxieties. Frame the AI as a tool to eliminate the drudgery they already dislike, a point that resonates powerfully with the findings of the Stanford HAI study.

Instead of a generic statement, be specific: "I know that everyone dreads the process of compiling the weekly sales report. It takes about five hours of our collective time each Monday. We are piloting a new AI tool that we believe can automate 80 percent of that process. My goal is to free up that time so we can focus on a more strategic project that we have all been wanting to tackle: a deep-dive analysis of our top competitors." This makes the benefit tangible and directly addresses a known pain point.

Third, you should appoint human champions. The Virgin Atlantic "AI Champion" apprenticeship is a brilliant model for this. By identifying and training employees from non-technical departments to become internal AI experts, the company is creating a network of trusted, relatable peers who can provide support and guidance. A team member is often more willing to ask a "dumb question" to a colleague than to a manager or an IT professional. These champions act as a vital bridge, translating the technical capabilities of the AI into the practical, day-to-day language of their department. They can host informal office hours, share best practices in a team chat, and act as a crucial feedback loop, bringing real-world user experiences back to the leadership team.

Section 2: The Leader as AI Translator and Ethical Steward

The introduction of AI into a team does more than just change the workflow; it fundamentally changes the role of the leader. As AI begins to automate many of the traditional tasks of management, such as tracking progress, generating reports, and even scheduling work, the leader's value shifts. You are no longer just the person who directs the work; you are the person who provides the context, the judgment, and the conscience for an increasingly complex human-machine system. This new role has two primary components: the leader as AI Translator and the leader as Ethical Steward.

As an AI Translator, your job is to bridge the gap between the abstract potential of the technology and the concrete reality of your team's work. Your team is likely being bombarded with a confusing mix of hype and fear from the outside world. Your role is to be the signal in the noise, the trusted curator who can filter the endless stream of new tools and trends and identify the few that are genuinely relevant and valuable to your team's specific mission. This does not mean you need to become a technical expert. It means you need to develop enough AI fluency to see the opportunities that others might miss. You need to be able to look at a frustrating, time-consuming process and ask, "Could an AI help us with this?" The Scaled Agile framework, a popular methodology for managing large-scale projects, advises that AI should be used to "enhance human abilities" by handling the routine tasks, thereby freeing people to focus on the more creative, judgment-driven work.[120] As a leader, you are the one who must identify those opportunities for enhancement.

This translation work is a continuous process. It involves staying current with the latest tools and techniques, as we discussed in the Power User Playbook, and then actively connecting those new capabilities to your team's specific challenges. For example, you might read about a new AI tool that is particularly good at analyzing customer feedback. As an AI Translator, you would not just forward the article with a note that says, "This looks interesting." You would do the translation work. You would design a small pilot project, a prompt sprint, to test the tool on your own customer data. You would frame the experiment in the language of business value: "I'd like to run a small test with a new tool that I believe could help us analyze the 1,000 open-ended survey responses we get each quarter. My hypothesis is that it could save us 20 hours of manual coding and help us spot emerging customer issues two weeks faster. I'm looking for two volunteers to help me run this experiment next Friday." This approach transforms a vague technological possibility into a specific, measurable business initiative. You are the catalyst, the one who brings the technology to life in a way that is directly relevant to your team's goals.

The second, and arguably more important, new role is that of the Ethical Steward. As AI becomes more powerful and autonomous, the leader's responsibility for ensuring that it is used in a fair, transparent, and responsible manner becomes paramount. As the author and strategist Charlene Li puts it, "leaders will become ethical stewards, ensuring AI aligns with our purpose, values and long-term goals... AI is a tool. How we choose to use it is where leadership matters."[121]

This is not a theoretical concern; it has profound practical implications. If your team is using an AI tool to help screen job candidates, you are responsible for ensuring that the tool is not perpetuating or even amplifying historical biases present in your company's past hiring data. An AI trained on a decade of data from a company that predominantly hired men for technical roles may learn to associate male-coded language with success, systematically down-ranking qualified female candidates. As the leader, you must be the one to ask the hard questions and demand transparency from the system.

If your team is using an AI to personalize marketing messages, you are responsible for ensuring that you are not creating manipulative or discriminatory experiences for your customers. An AI might discover that a certain demographic is particularly susceptible to messaging that creates a sense of scarcity and anxiety. A purely data-driven approach might exploit this vulnerability to maximize sales. As the Ethical Steward, you must be the one to draw the line between effective personalization and unethical manipulation.

If your team is using an AI to summarize customer service calls, you are responsible for ensuring that the privacy of those customers is protected. This means establishing clear guidelines about what data can be used, how it is anonymized, and who has access to it.

Being an effective Ethical Steward requires a new set of leadership skills. It requires the courage to ask tough questions of your technology vendors and your own IT department. It requires critical thinking to question the output of an AI, to ask "What data was this trained on?" and "What biases might be embedded in this recommendation?" It also requires a deep and unwavering commitment to your organization's values. This is a proactive, not a reactive, role. It involves working with your team to create a simple "Team AI Charter," a set of guiding principles for the responsible use of these tools, before a problem arises.

One author on the topic of leadership captured this idea perfectly: "AI is not a competitor to human greatness but a collaborator. It can analyze vast data, reveal hidden patterns, automate tasks and augment intelligence: freeing leaders to focus more on vision, empathy, innovation and human connection... AI is a tool, but you are the heart. Empathy, compassion, intuition, humor, vulnerability: these are the gifts only human leaders can bring."[122]

This is the ultimate redefinition of the leader's role. As AI handles more of the management tasks (e.g., the tracking, the reporting, the scheduling) you are freed to focus on the art of leadership. The data supports this shift. A recent survey found that 83 percent of executives believe that human skills like ethical judgment and empathy will become even more vital with the rise of AI.[123] Your most important job in the age of AI is to be the most human person in the room.

Conclusion

The age of AI does not mark the end of leadership; it marks the beginning of a new and more human-centric era of it. The old model of the manager as a director of tasks and a controller of information is becoming obsolete, automated by the very technology that many fear. The value of a leader who simply relays instructions from above and checks to see if the work is done is rapidly approaching zero. That is a function an AI can perform with far greater efficiency. What is emerging in its place is a new model of the leader as a coach, a strategist, and a conscience. The skills that now define effective leadership are the very pillars of the Human Edge we have been exploring throughout this book. It is the Humanity to manage an augmented team with empathy, the Thinking to act as a savvy AI Translator, the Adaptability to guide your team through constant change, and the Creativity to envision new and better ways of working.

The central takeaway is that modern leadership is about being a guide for transformation, not a gatekeeper of old processes. Your role is to create an environment of psychological safety where your team feels empowered to experiment, to learn, and to partner with this powerful new technology. It is about building a culture where asking for help with a new tool is seen as a sign of strength, not weakness, and where collaborative problem-solving is the default response to any new challenge. By doing so, you are not just future-proofing your team's skills; you are future-proofing your own.

These leadership capabilities, the ability to foster trust, to communicate a clear vision, and to act as an ethical steward, are the ultimate durable skills. They are the foundation for a long and resilient career, one that evolves with the technology rather than being replaced by it. These are the skills that will allow you to play the long game, a topic we will explore in the final part of this book.

PART IV: FUTURE-SELF: BUILD A CAREER THAT EVOLVES WITH YOU

Chapter 14: Design a Career That Won't Expire

Introduction

When Tanya Brno was laid off from her job in user experience design, she faced the same daunting question as millions of other professionals caught in the crosscurrents of a volatile market: What now? The traditional path would have been to polish her resume, update her LinkedIn profile, and begin the arduous process of applying for another full-time corporate role, seeking to replace the single source of income she had lost. Instead, she chose a different path, one that is becoming increasingly common in a world of profound uncertainty. She did not look for another job; she built a portfolio. Today, her professional life is a dynamic mix of freelance UX design projects, performances as a professional aerial acrobat, and co-running a bamboo nursery. It is an unconventional combination, but it is also a powerful model of modern career resilience.[124]

Brno's story is not an outlier; it is a postcard from the future of work. Her approach represents a strategic decision to build an "antifragile" career, one that does not just resist shocks but actually gets stronger from them. By diversifying her skills and income streams, she has designed a professional life that is not dependent on the whims of a single employer or the stability of a single industry. The concept of a single, linear career, a predictable, 40-year climb up a single corporate ladder, is a relic of a bygone era. It was a model built for a world of stability and predictability, a world that no longer exists. For much of the 20th century, the social contract was clear: you offered a company your loyalty, and in return, it offered you a lifetime of security.

The relentless pace of technological change, driven by artificial intelligence, has shattered that model. AI is not just another tool that makes us more efficient at our old jobs. It is a force that is actively automating the cognitive tasks that were once the exclusive domain of the human knowledge worker. This final part of the book is about how to thrive in that new reality. It is about moving beyond the tactics of surviving the next few years and adopting the long-term strategies for building a career that can evolve, adapt, and renew itself over a lifetime. This chapter will show you how to design a career that will not expire. We will explore the new imperative of continuous reinvention and introduce the portfolio mindset as the new foundation for professional stability.

Section 1: The End of the Linear Career: Reinvent Early and Often

The idea of a "job for life" has been fading for decades, but the AI revolution has accelerated its demise into a sudden and definitive end. The new organizing principle of a successful professional life is not loyalty to a single company or mastery of a single skill set, but a capacity for continuous reinvention. The data on this cultural and economic shift is unambiguous, painting a clear picture of a workforce in motion, actively seeking to outrun the pace of technological change.

A late 2024 survey revealed a startling statistic: a majority of U.S. job seekers, 56 percent, reported that they wanted to switch to a new industry altogether. This is a dramatic increase from the roughly one-third of workers who expressed the same desire before 2019.[125] This is not just a sign of post-pandemic restlessness; it is a signal of a fundamental break in the traditional career contract. This mass desire for change is a strategic response to the perceived vulnerability of entire sectors. Professionals are looking at the landscape, performing their own informal "creep risk" audits, and concluding that the safest move is not to dig in their heels, but to find higher ground. They are no longer looking for a predictable path; they are actively seeking change, driven by a combination of burnout in their current fields, a search for more meaningful work, and a pragmatic recognition that the industries that seem safe today may not be safe tomorrow.

This desire for reinvention is not just a personal preference; it is becoming a market necessity. The skills that are valuable today are becoming obsolete at a faster rate than at any other time in history. The World Economic Forum projects that, on average, 39 percent of a worker's core skills will be disrupted or rendered outdated by 2030.[126] This means that in less than a decade, nearly half of what you know how to do may no longer be relevant. A report from the Boston Consulting Group paints an even starker picture, noting that the "average half-life of skills is now less than five years, and half that in some tech fields."[127]

The concept of a "half-life of skills" is a powerful one. Think of a professional skill like a radioactive isotope; it has a period of peak potency, but over time, its value decays. If the half-life of a technical skill is just two and a half years, it means that a software developer who stops learning today will be only a quarter as effective in five years. For a mid-career professional who graduated from college fifteen years ago, the initial "charge" of their formal education has almost completely decayed. This relentless depreciation of skill value creates a powerful imperative for continuous learning and adaptation. It means that the old model of front-loading your education (i.e., getting a degree at 22 and then coasting on that knowledge for 40 years) is a recipe for obsolescence.

The practical implication of this is that you must plan to reinvent your career in cycles of roughly five years. This does not necessarily mean a dramatic, industry-switching pivot every five years, like the one Amit Sharma made from QA to machine learning. A reinvention can also be a "micro-pivot," a more subtle but equally strategic shift. It is the process of adding a new, adjacent skill set that fundamentally redefines your value proposition. For example, a graphic designer who adds skills in motion graphics and video editing becomes a multimedia storyteller, a far more resilient role than a static image creator. A writer who masters SEO strategy and data analysis becomes a content strategist, capable of not just creating content but also proving its business impact. A project manager who becomes certified in change management and AI ethics becomes a transformation leader, a role of increasing importance in any large organization.

This new reality requires a profound psychological shift. The linear career path provided a sense of identity and security. Your job title was a shorthand for who you were and where you stood in the professional hierarchy. The new model of continuous reinvention requires you to detach your identity from your job title and attach it instead to your underlying skills and your capacity for growth. You are no longer a "Marketing Manager"; you are a professional who is skilled in communication, strategy, and customer psychology, and you are currently applying those skills in a marketing context. This subtle reframing is the key to the psychological flexibility required to navigate a world where your context will be constantly changing. The end of the linear career is not a tragedy to be mourned. It is a new game with a new set of rules, and for those who are willing to play it, it offers a new and more dynamic form of freedom.

Section 2: The Portfolio Mindset: Your New Safety Net

For generations, the primary safety net for a professional career was a stable, full-time job at a reputable company. The goal was to find a good employer and hold on, weathering economic downturns under the relative protection of a large organization. That safety net has frayed to the point of breaking. In a world of rapid technological change, corporate restructuring, and global competition, the single-job model has become a source of profound fragility. Placing your entire professional and financial security in the hands of one employer is no longer a safe bet; it is a high-risk gamble. The new safety net, the modern model for stability, is the portfolio.

Adopting a portfolio mindset means shifting your thinking from "I have a job" to "I manage a portfolio of skills, projects, and income streams." It is the mindset of an investor, who knows that diversification is the key to managing risk and maximizing long-term returns. Tanya Brno's story is a perfect illustration of this principle in action. When she lost her single source of income, her UX design job, she did not replace it with another single source. She diversified. By building a portfolio that combined freelance design work, her passion for aerial performance, and a stake in a small business, she created a career that was far more resilient than the one she had before. A downturn in the tech industry might affect her freelance design work, but it has no impact on the demand for aerial performances or bamboo plants. This is the portfolio mindset in its most literal form: a collection of distinct and uncorrelated assets that provide stability in a volatile world.

This is not a niche strategy for a few creative freelancers. It is a mainstream trend that is reshaping the very definition of a career. A 2024 survey from Bankrate found that over a third of Americans, 36 percent, now have a side hustle, earning extra income beyond their primary job.[128] This is not just about making ends meet; it is a strategic choice. As career expert Dr. Gabby Burlacu noted in 2025, many professionals, particularly those in younger generations who have grown up in an era of economic uncertainty, now view portfolio work as a deliberate hedge against financial risk.[129] They are choosing to build their own safety nets rather than relying on the fraying one offered by traditional employment.

At its core, the portfolio mindset requires a fundamental shift from thinking in terms of titles to thinking in terms of skills. A job title is a label assigned to you by an employer. It is temporary and context-dependent. A skill, on the other hand, is an asset that you own. It is portable and can be applied in a wide variety of contexts. The professional who identifies as a "Senior Marketing Manager at Company X" has a fragile identity. If Company X has a round of layoffs, that identity is threatened. The professional who identifies as "a strategist who is skilled in communication, data analysis, and brand storytelling" has a resilient identity. If her current role is eliminated, she can take that portfolio of skills and apply it in a new context: as a freelancer, a consultant, a founder, or an employee at a different company.

This is why transferable, human-centric skills are the most valuable currency in a portfolio career. While technical skills are important, they often have a short half-life and can be specific to a particular tool or platform. The durable skills of the C.H.A.T. model, however, are universally applicable. The ability to communicate clearly, for example, is just as valuable when you are pitching a freelance client as it is when you are presenting to a corporate board. It is no surprise that a recent LinkedIn analysis identified communication as the number one most in-demand skill in the global job market.[130] It is the master skill that allows you to articulate the value of all your other skills.

Adopting a portfolio mindset is an empowering act. It reframes you as the CEO of your own career, You, Inc. You are no longer a passive employee, but an active manager of a diverse and evolving set of professional assets. This mindset is the foundation for the practical, hands-on work of building a career that will not expire.

Section 3: Building Your "Career Ecosystem": A Practical Guide

Thinking like a portfolio manager is the first step. The next is to become an active builder, to deliberately construct a professional life that is designed for resilience and renewal. The goal is to create a personal "career ecosystem," a dynamic and interconnected system of skills, projects, brand assets, and networks that work together to sustain your growth and create a steady flow of new opportunities. This is not something that happens by accident; it is the result of a series of intentional practices. Here are the five key practices for building your own self-renewing career ecosystem.

1. Think Skills, Not Jobs

The foundational practice is to deconstruct your professional identity into a portfolio of skills. This means looking past your current job title and creating a detailed inventory of your capabilities. A great way to do this is to create a "skill tree," much like the ones found in video games. Your core, foundational skills (like communication or problem-solving) form the trunk. Branching off from there are your more specialized skills (like data analysis, project management, or graphic design). This exercise helps you to see your career not as a linear path, but as a collection of assets that can be combined in new and interesting ways.

This "skills-first" approach is not just a personal branding exercise; it is a reflection of a major shift in the way companies themselves are thinking about talent. A growing number of major employers are moving toward a skills-first hiring model, where they prioritize a candidate's demonstrated capabilities over their formal credentials. The retail giant Walmart, for example, is a founding member of the Skills-First Workforce Initiative. The company is actively removing college degree requirements for many of its corporate roles and has invested over $1 billion in skills-based training programs for its employees. One of its flagship programs, "Associate to Technician," trains hourly associates for higher-paying technical roles with no degree required, creating a powerful internal pipeline for in-demand jobs.[131] Research has shown that this approach is not just good for social mobility; it is good for business. One study found that companies that adopt skills-first hiring can expand their available talent pool by a factor of ten, all while improving employee retention.[132] By thinking in terms of skills, you are aligning yourself with this powerful market trend.

2. Build a Personal Brand

In a portfolio career, you are the product. Your personal brand is the story you tell about that product. It is the narrative that connects the seemingly disparate parts of your portfolio into a coherent and compelling whole. Your brand is not about creating a fake or overly polished persona; it is about being intentional in how you communicate your value to the world.

The most important asset in your personal brand is your portfolio of work, the tangible proof we discussed in Chapter 7. This is your collection of case studies, projects, and results that demonstrate your skills in action. This portfolio should have a central home, such as a personal website or a well-curated LinkedIn profile. From there, you can use the "portfolio stacking" technique to share your insights and expertise across different platforms, building a reputation as a knowledgeable and valuable contributor in your field.

3. Plan 5-Year Reinventions

A resilient ecosystem is not static; it is constantly evolving. The practice of planning five-year reinventions is about building this process of evolution directly into your career strategy. It is a commitment to proactively disrupting yourself before the market does it for you. As one futurist writing for the Harvard Business Review described her own process, every four years she deliberately "sheds a professional skin and starts fresh."[133] This does not mean she abandons her past experience, but that she consciously chooses to enter a new phase of learning and growth, adding a new and significant branch to her skill tree.

Your five-year reinvention plan should be a living document. At the beginning of each cycle, you should go through the process of identifying a "North Star" for the next five years, as we discussed in Chapter 10. What new skills do you want to acquire? What new types of projects do you want to work on? What new industry do you want to learn about? By making this a regular, scheduled practice, you transform reinvention from a panicked reaction to a calm, deliberate, and empowering process of growth.

4. Adopt Flexibility Frameworks

To guide your reinvention cycles, it is helpful to have a set of mental models or frameworks for exploration. These are not rigid rules, but flexible guides for thinking about your career in a more creative and expansive way.

One popular framework is the Japanese concept of Ikigai, which is often translated as "a reason for being." It is found at the intersection of four questions: What do you love? What are you good at? What can you be paid for? and What does the world need? By using these four questions as a lens for brainstorming, you can identify potential career paths that align with your passions, your talents, your financial needs, and your desire for meaningful impact.[134]

Another powerful approach is the "design thinking" framework for careers, popularized by Bill Burnett and Dave Evans in their book Designing Your Life. The core idea is to treat your career not as a problem to be solved, but as a design to be prototyped. Instead of trying to figure out the one perfect path, you run small, low-cost experiments to test different possibilities. As the career strategist Justin Lokitz explains, you can "prototype a career change" by finding someone who is already doing the work that interests you and offering to help them with a small project, often for free. This "ride-along" approach is a low-risk way to get a real feel for a new role before you make a full commitment.[135]

5. Leverage Learning Platforms

The engine that powers your entire career ecosystem is a commitment to continuous learning. In a world where the half-life of skills is shrinking, your ability to learn quickly and effectively is your most important meta-skill. Fortunately, the ecosystem of online learning platforms has made it easier and more affordable than ever to acquire new skills.

The practice here is to build a continuous learning loop into your professional life. This means treating each job and each project as an opportunity for both execution and education. It means setting aside a small, consistent budget of time and money for your own professional development. As LinkedIn's 2024 report on workplace trends noted, "continuous learning is critical" for navigating the modern world of work.[136] This might mean subscribing to a platform like Coursera or LinkedIn Learning, joining a professional community that offers workshops and webinars, or simply dedicating a few hours each week to working through a free online tutorial. The key is to make learning a regular, non-negotiable habit, like exercise or saving for retirement. It is the investment you make in ensuring that your career ecosystem is always growing, always adapting, and never at risk of becoming obsolete.

Conclusion

The architecture of a 20th-century career, with its promise of a linear ascent up a stable corporate ladder, is no longer structurally sound in the turbulent environment of the 21st century. The foundational assumption of stability has been replaced by the reality of constant change. To build a career that will not expire, you must become a new kind of architect, one who designs for flexibility, resilience, and continuous evolution. The goal is no longer to find a safe harbor in a single job, but to build a vessel that is seaworthy enough to navigate any storm.

This is the purpose of the portfolio mindset. By deliberately constructing a personal "career ecosystem", a dynamic, self-renewing system of skills, projects, brand assets, and networks, you create a new and more durable form of professional security. Through deliberate practices, from planning five-year reinventions to building a personal brand and thinking in terms of skills rather than titles, you can construct this new foundation for your professional life. This ecosystem is your external strategy, the tangible structure that makes you adaptable and keeps you relevant in a volatile market.

But building this external scaffolding is only half of the equation. A resilient structure requires an equally strong internal core. The constant pressure to learn, adapt, and reinvent can be psychologically taxing. It demands a high level of emotional energy, a tolerance for ambiguity, and the ability to bounce back from the inevitable setbacks and failures that accompany a life of continuous growth. This external strategy for career design must be supported by an internal strategy for self-management. Building a portfolio of skills is not enough; you must also cultivate the emotional stamina to deploy those skills effectively, year after year. Before we can play the long game, we must first master the inner game. The next chapter will show you how to build the emotional stamina required to stay human and stay relevant.

Chapter 15: Stay Human, Stay Relevant

Introduction

The modern professional world is a landscape of relentless change. New technologies emerge, industries pivot, and the skills that were in high demand yesterday can become obsolete tomorrow. This constant churn creates a significant psychological burden, a low-grade, chronic stress that permeates our working lives. A 2024 LinkedIn survey found that nearly 64 percent of professionals feel overwhelmed by the sheer pace of change in the workplace.[137] This is a quiet but pervasive epidemic of professional anxiety. It is the feeling of being perpetually behind, of running on a treadmill that is constantly accelerating, with the fear that a misstep could mean being thrown off completely. The external strategies we discussed in the previous chapter, building a portfolio career, planning five-year reinventions, and leveraging learning platforms, are the necessary architectural plans for building a resilient career. But a brilliant architectural plan is useless if the builder is exhausted, anxious, and burned out.

An external strategy for career design must be supported by an equally robust internal strategy for self-management. The most sophisticated career ecosystem will fail if the person at its center lacks the inner fortitude to sustain it. The constant need to learn, adapt, and perform in an environment of high uncertainty is not just a strategic challenge; it is an emotional one. This chapter is your guide to building that internal foundation. It is about developing the psychological tools and mental models you need to not just survive, but thrive in an environment of constant flux. We will move from the "what" of career design to the "how" of personal resilience. This is not about feel-good platitudes; it is a practical playbook for cultivating the emotional stamina that is now as vital as any technical skill. In an age where machines are becoming more intelligent, our ability to stay grounded, focused, and human is our ultimate competitive advantage.

Section 1: Cultivating Emotional Stamina

In the world of athletics, no one would expect a marathon runner to succeed based on raw talent alone. We understand that victory in an endurance event requires a specific and highly developed quality: stamina. It is the ability to withstand prolonged physical stress, to push through discomfort, and to maintain focus and motivation over a long and grueling course. In the 21st-century world of work, we are all now endurance athletes. The sprint of a single, linear career has been replaced by the marathon of continuous reinvention, and success in this new event requires a new kind of fitness: emotional stamina.

Emotional stamina is the psychological capacity to navigate uncertainty, to bounce back from setbacks, and to sustain your motivation and sense of purpose through the inevitable ups and downs of a long and non-linear career. It is the inner resilience that allows you to see a disruption not as a threat that triggers panic, but as a challenge that sparks curiosity. It is the engine that powers the lifelong learning and adaptation that a future-proof career demands. Without it, even the best-laid career plans will crumble under the weight of chronic stress and burnout. Cultivating this quality is not a passive process; it is an active practice built on two foundational pillars: adopting a growth mindset and clarifying your personal mission.

The foundational operating system for emotional stamina is the adoption of a growth mindset. This concept, developed by Stanford psychologist Carol Dweck, is one of the most powerful mental models for navigating a world of change. Dweck's research identifies two core mindsets through which we view our abilities. A fixed mindset is the belief that our intelligence, talents, and capabilities are static, inborn traits. From this perspective, a challenge is a test that you either pass or fail, and failure is a verdict on your inherent worth. A growth mindset, on the other hand, is the belief that our abilities can be developed through dedication, effort, and a willingness to learn. From this perspective, a challenge is not a test, but an opportunity, and failure is not a verdict, but a valuable piece of feedback.

Consider how two professionals with these different mindsets might react to the introduction of a new AI tool that automates a part of their job. The professional with a fixed mindset sees the tool as a threat. Their internal monologue is filled with fear: "This machine is better at this than I am. I'm going to be obsolete. I'll never be able to learn this new technology; I'm just not a 'tech person.'" This mindset leads to resistance, anxiety, and a defensive posture that ultimately accelerates their irrelevance. They avoid the new tool, their skills stagnate, and their fear becomes a self-fulfilling prophecy.

The professional with a growth mindset sees the exact same event through a different lens. Their internal monologue is one of curiosity and opportunity: "This is interesting. This tool can handle the boring, repetitive part of my job, which will free me up to focus on the more strategic challenges. I'm not sure how to use it yet, but I'm confident I can learn. This is a chance to add a new skill to my portfolio." This mindset leads to engagement, experimentation, and growth. As one psychology expert explains, "Having a growth mindset will allow one to see discomfort not as a cause for stress, but as an opportunity to learn and grow."[138] This reframing of discomfort is the core mechanism of emotional stamina. It is the ability to lean into a challenge rather than shrink from it.

While a growth mindset provides the "how" of navigating challenges, a strong sense of purpose provides the "why." A personal mission statement is a powerful tool for cultivating this sense of purpose. It is a concise declaration of your core values and the impact you want to have on the world, independent of any specific job title or employer. It is your personal North Star, the anchor that holds you steady in turbulent waters. Your job can be taken from you, but your purpose cannot.

Crafting a personal mission statement is an exercise in self-reflection. It involves asking yourself a series of deep questions: What are the problems I am most passionate about solving? When do I feel most energized and alive in my work? What are my unique, core strengths? What legacy do I want to leave? Your mission statement should be a synthesis of these reflections. It is not a description of what you do, but of who you are and what you stand for. For example, a generic job description might be "I am a software engineer." A purpose-driven mission statement might be "My mission is to use my skills in technology to build tools that empower creative people to share their stories with the world." This sense of a higher purpose provides a deep well of motivation that can sustain you through the difficult and often frustrating process of reinvention. Psychological research has shown that a strong sense of purpose is a powerful buffer against stress and a key ingredient in long-term well-being.[139]

These two concepts, a growth mindset and a personal mission statement, are the twin engines of emotional stamina. The growth mindset is the belief that you can change and adapt. The mission statement is the reason why you should. Together, they create a powerful internal guidance system that allows you to navigate the external chaos of the modern career with a sense of agency, confidence, and enduring purpose.

Section 2: The Psychology of Reinvention: It's Never Too Late

For the mid-career professional, the greatest barrier to reinvention is often not a lack of opportunity, but a psychological wall built from years of accumulated identity. The thought of starting over can be terrifying, not just because of the financial risk, but because it threatens our very sense of self. We have spent decades defining ourselves by our work. The question "What do you do?" is a proxy for "Who are you?" in many cultures. When your answer has been "I am a lawyer" or "I am an accountant" for twenty years, the prospect of no longer being that person can feel like a form of ego death. This is the trap of the fixed professional identity, and it is the single most powerful force that keeps people stuck in careers that are no longer fulfilling or viable. This identity is reinforced by years of social validation, a specific professional network, and the powerful cognitive bias of the sunk cost fallacy: the feeling that you have invested too much time and energy in one path to possibly change course now.

Overcoming this trap requires a deliberate and courageous act of psychological reframing. It begins with the understanding that your skills are transferable, even if your job title is not. Patti Thull is a powerful example of this. After a long and successful career in corporate communications, she found herself at a crossroads at age 50. Instead of clinging to the familiar, she made the bold decision to launch a new career as a freelance writer. The key to her successful pivot was a fundamental shift in her self-perception. "I realized my skills were transferable and my life wasn't over," she explained. "It was just entering a new chapter."[140] She understood that the core skills she had honed for decades, the ability to craft a clear message, to understand an audience, to manage complex projects, and to navigate corporate politics, were not limited to a corporate context. They were portable assets that could be the foundation for a new and more fulfilling professional life. She deconstructed her identity from a job title into a portfolio of durable human skills.

This idea of a non-linear, evolving career is moving from an unconventional choice to the new mainstream. A 2024 analysis in Forbes powerfully articulated this shift, coining the advice to "don't settle, squiggle."[141] The old metaphor for a career was a ladder, a single, linear ascent to a predetermined peak within a single organization or industry. The new, more accurate metaphor is a squiggle, a path with twists, turns, and even moments that seem to go backward, but which is ultimately a journey of exploration and growth. The research supports this new model. The same Forbes analysis noted that people who change jobs in midlife often end up better paid, more engaged, and working longer by choice than those who stay put. They are more likely to be employed and satisfied in their 60s, suggesting that reinvention is a powerful engine for long-term career vitality.

This is not a niche phenomenon. A UK study found that a full third of professionals between the ages of 45 and 54 are actively planning to change their careers before they retire.[142] They are part of a growing movement of mid-career professionals who are choosing to be the authors of their own second acts rather than passively accepting the final chapters that their old career paths had written for them. The most common thread among those who succeed is the ability to overcome the fear of being a beginner again. This requires redefining what it means to be a beginner. An early-career professional is a true novice, starting with a blank slate. A mid-career professional who pivots is a "wise beginner." You may be new to a specific tool or a particular industry's jargon, but you bring with you a deep reservoir of what we have called the "wisdom layer": the contextual knowledge, the political savvy, and the nuanced understanding of human nature that can only be acquired through years of experience.

This wisdom allows you to learn faster, to see patterns that a true novice would miss, and to avoid the common mistakes that can derail a project. An experienced manager pivoting into a new industry, for example, may not know the specific technical details on day one, but she already knows how to run an effective meeting, how to build consensus among a skeptical team, how to manage a budget, and how to communicate with senior leadership. These are the meta-skills that are often far more valuable than any specific piece of technical knowledge. The psychology of reinvention, therefore, is not about erasing your past. It is about integrating it. It is about having the confidence to say, "I am not just a banker. I am a problem-solver with deep expertise in financial systems, and I can apply that skill to a new challenge in the healthcare technology sector." It is about seeing your career not as a series of disconnected jobs, but as a coherent story of evolving skills and accumulating wisdom. This narrative lens gives you a sense of agency and continuity, even as the external form of your work changes.

Section 3: Practical Habits for Resilience and Well-Being

The marathon of continuous reinvention is demanding. Without a deliberate practice of self-management, the constant pressure to learn and adapt can easily lead to burnout. Staying current in a fast-moving world requires more than just drive; it requires a sustainable set of habits that protect your energy, your focus, and your mental health. This is the practical, day-to-day work of building emotional stamina. Here are five key habits for staying human and relevant without sacrificing your well-being.

1. Practice Resilience Rituals

Resilience is not an inborn trait; it is a skill that can be cultivated through consistent practice. A resilience ritual is an intentional, repeated habit designed to strengthen your psychological core. This goes beyond simply "managing stress" and moves toward proactively building your capacity to handle it. A powerful and simple ritual is a daily or weekly practice of journaling. At the end of each day, take five minutes to write down a challenge you faced and how you dealt with it. This practice of reflective writing does two things. It helps you to process the stress of the day, and more importantly, it creates a written record of your own efficacy. When you look back over a month of these entries, you have concrete evidence of your ability to overcome obstacles, which is a powerful antidote to the feeling of being overwhelmed.

Another key ritual is building and maintaining a strong support network. Psychological research consistently links strong social and professional support systems with higher career adaptability.[143] This means scheduling regular, non-transactional conversations with mentors, peers, and friends who can offer perspective, encouragement, and a safe space to be vulnerable. This is your personal board of directors, the people who can remind you of your strengths when you are feeling doubtful and challenge you when you are becoming complacent. This should be a structured practice, not a haphazard one. You might schedule a recurring monthly call with a small group of trusted peers where the only agenda is to discuss career challenges and share advice.

2. Curate Your Learning (A "Healthy Information Diet")

In an age of information overload, the undisciplined consumption of news and social media is a direct path to anxiety and burnout. The constant stream of headlines about AI breakthroughs and industry disruptions can create a sense of perpetual panic. A power user of information does not try to drink from the firehose; they build a filtration system. This is the practice of curating a "healthy information diet." As LinkedIn's career team advises, "By staying up-to-date with the latest news and insights from trusted experts...you can avoid feeling overwhelmed and more in control."[144]

This means being ruthlessly selective about your sources. Choose one or two high-quality industry newsletters, one or two podcasts, and a small handful of insightful thinkers to follow.

Unsubscribe from everything else. Then, be intentional about when you consume this information. Instead of letting it interrupt you throughout the day, time-box your learning. You might dedicate the first 30 minutes of your morning to reading your newsletters and then log off for the rest of the day. This practice of "focused upskilling", choosing one skill to learn or one topic to follow at a time, is far more effective and less stressful than frantically trying to know everything all at once. It is a shift from the "just-in-case" learning of the past (hoarding knowledge in case it might be useful one day) to the "just-in-time" learning of the present (acquiring the specific knowledge you need for the challenge at hand).

3. Set Digital Detox Boundaries

The human brain is not designed to be in a state of constant, low-grade stimulation. It needs periods of rest and unstructured time to consolidate learning, to think creatively, and to recover from the cognitive load of a demanding workday. In a world of remote work and constant connectivity, the boundaries between work and life have become dangerously blurred. Setting deliberate digital detox boundaries is no longer a luxury; it is a strategic necessity for long-term performance.

This can take many forms. It might mean establishing a firm "no-email-after-7-PM" rule. It could be the practice of a "digital sabbath," where you put your phone and laptop away for a full day on the weekend. It could be as simple as taking a 20-minute walk in the middle of the day without your phone. These periods of disconnection are not a sign of laziness; they are a vital part of the recovery process that prevents burnout and allows you to return to your work with renewed energy and a clearer perspective. Cognitive science tells us that our brains need to enter the "default mode network" to make creative connections, a state that is suppressed by constant external stimuli. Your best ideas will often come not when you are staring at a screen, but when you are letting your mind wander.

4. Reframe Self-Talk in Uncertainty

The internal narrative you tell yourself has a profound impact on your ability to navigate challenges. When faced with uncertainty, your self-talk can either be a source of paralyzing anxiety or a wellspring of resilient confidence. The practice here is to become the conscious director of your own inner monologue. This is the practical, moment-to-moment application of the growth mindset.

When you catch yourself engaging in a fixed-mindset narrative, such as "I'll never be able to learn this new software; it's too complicated," you must actively reframe it. The reframed, growth-mindset version would be, "This new software looks challenging, and I'll probably make some mistakes at first, but I'm confident I can figure it out, just like I've figured out new things in the past." This is not about empty positive thinking; it is about grounding your self-talk in the reality of your past successes. As one CEO wrote in an essay on leadership, "Embracing discomfort is one of the best ways for leaders to become more adaptable and resilient... Moving through uncomfortable situations builds the confidence that leads to resilience... and proves to ourselves that we are capable of learning new skills and overcoming new challenges."[145]

5. Connect with Purpose

The final and most powerful habit for building emotional stamina is to regularly connect your daily work to your larger sense of purpose, your personal mission statement. In the grind of a busy week, it is easy to lose sight of the "why" behind your work. This can lead to a sense of alienation and burnout. The practice of connecting with purpose is about deliberately reminding yourself of the impact you want to have.

This can be done through a simple weekly reflection. At the end of each week, ask yourself: "Where did I make a positive impact this week? How did my work connect to my personal mission?" This practice reframes your work not as a series of tasks to be completed, but as a series of opportunities to live out your values. This is directly supported by the findings of the Stanford HAI study, which showed that professionals have a deep-seated need to protect the "human touch" and their sense of "agency" in their work.[146] By consciously connecting your daily actions to a larger purpose, you are actively nurturing that sense of agency and reinforcing the meaningfulness of your contribution. This is the ultimate source of the emotional fuel you will need to run the marathon of a long and evolving career.

Conclusion

The most sophisticated career portfolio in the world is worthless without the psychological resilience to manage it. The external strategies for reinvention that we explored in the previous chapter are demanding. They require you to live in a state of continuous learning, to embrace uncertainty, and to navigate the inevitable setbacks that come with a non-linear path. This is not just a strategic challenge; it is an emotional marathon. The practices outlined in this chapter are your training plan for that marathon. They are the tools for building the emotional stamina that is now as vital to your professional survival as any technical skill.

The core takeaway is that your internal state is not a soft, secondary concern; it is a hard, strategic asset. Your ability to cultivate a growth mindset, to anchor yourself in a personal mission, and to build sustainable habits for well-being is what will determine your capacity to execute your long-term career vision. In a world increasingly populated by intelligent machines, our humanity, our ability to adapt, to find meaning, to connect with purpose, and to bounce back from failure, is not a liability to be overcome, but a core advantage to be nurtured. The Stanford study confirmed that professionals are instinctively fighting to protect their sense of agency and human touch at work, and the habits in this chapter are the practical means of fortifying that ground.

You now have the external architecture for your career in the form of a portfolio ecosystem and the internal operating system of emotional stamina to run it effectively. You have a plan for what to build and the inner resilience to see that plan through. With this complete toolkit, a robust external strategy supported by an equally robust internal one, you are no longer just reacting to the future. You are prepared to actively shape it. You are now ready to play the long game.

Chapter 16: The Long Game: Building a Career That Lasts

Introduction

A veteran product manager at a major fintech company found herself at the center of her organization's AI transformation. For years, her role had been a careful balance of technical oversight and market strategy. She was an expert in the data, the A-B tests, and the key performance indicators that drove her product's success. But as the company integrated sophisticated AI systems, she noticed a profound shift. The routine analytical tasks that had once consumed a significant portion of her time, running A-B tests, analyzing user data, generating performance reports, were now being handled with incredible speed and accuracy by algorithms. She had a choice. She could have doubled down on her technical skills, trying to become the company's foremost expert on the new AI tools, competing with the machine on its own terms. This was the path many of her colleagues were taking, a frantic race to stay technically current. Instead, she chose to play the long game.

She recognized that the AI was a powerful tool for answering "what" questions: what is the user retention rate, what is the most effective call to action? But it was far less capable of answering the "why" and "so what" questions. Why are users dropping off at this specific point in the journey? So what if we increase the retention rate by two percent if it comes at the cost of long-term customer trust? She deliberately pivoted her focus away from the mechanics of the data and toward the meaning behind it. She began spending more of her time on the deeply human work that the AI could not do. She conducted more in-depth customer interviews, seeking to understand the emotional drivers and unmet needs that were not visible in the quantitative data. She dedicated more time to mentoring the junior product managers on her team, sharing the hard-won wisdom and contextual knowledge she had accumulated over her career. And she focused on shaping the long-term product vision, translating the AI's analytical output into a compelling strategic narrative that could inspire her team and persuade senior leadership.

She did not abandon the technology; she orchestrated it. She was no longer just a player in the orchestra, trying to play her instrument faster and more accurately than anyone else. She was becoming the conductor, interpreting the music, guiding the entire ensemble, and ensuring that the final performance was not just technically perfect, but also emotionally resonant. She became known not as the most technical product manager, but as the wisest. She was the "AI translator," the indispensable human who could bridge the gap between the machine's powerful but narrow intelligence and the complex, messy reality of the business. Her career did not just survive the AI transition; it flourished because of it. She had mastered the long game.

This final chapter is about how you can do the same. The strategies we have discussed so far, from building your Human Edge to designing a portfolio career, are the foundational elements of a resilient professional life. Now, we will synthesize these ideas into a coherent, long-term philosophy for building a career that does not just last, but that becomes more valuable and more meaningful over time. We will explore the dangerous trap of chasing fleeting technical skills and make the definitive case for why your most durable assets are, and always will be, your human strengths.

Section 1: The Trap of "Tech Tricks": Why Durable Skills Matter Most

In a world of rapid technological change, it is tempting to believe that the key to career security is to constantly chase the next hot technical skill. The logic seems simple: if the world is being rebuilt with a new set of tools, then the most valuable people will be the ones who are the best at using those tools. This leads to a frantic, anxiety-driven scramble to learn the latest programming language, master the newest software platform, or become an expert in the most popular AI model. The allure of the tech trick is its promise of a quick fix, a tangible certificate or a new line on your resume that seems to guarantee immediate relevance. This is the trap of "tech tricks," and it is a short-term game that you are destined to lose.

The fundamental problem with a career strategy built solely on specific technical skills is that those skills have a rapidly shrinking half-life. As we discussed in Chapter 14, executives now estimate that in many fields, half of all skills will be outdated within just a few years.[147] This is a brutal reality. The specific AI prompting technique that is in high demand today could be rendered obsolete tomorrow by a new user interface that makes prompting easier for everyone. The programming language that is the gold standard this year could be a legacy language in five years. Building your entire professional identity on a foundation of these fleeting skills is like building a house on shifting sand.

195

We are already seeing clear evidence of this phenomenon in the job market. For years, the role of the software developer was seen as one of the most secure and lucrative careers of the digital age. But in 2023, something shifted. As generative AI became increasingly proficient at writing, debugging, and explaining code, job postings for software developers fell by a staggering 65 percent.[148] This does not mean that the need for people who can build software has vanished. It means that the value proposition of the role is changing. The market is becoming saturated with the ability to simply write code, a task that AI can now perform at a high level. The value is shifting away from the mechanical act of coding and toward the more durable, human skills that surround it. The value is now in the ability to sit with a frustrated client and translate their vague complaint into a clear technical specification, the creativity to design an elegant solution to a novel problem, and the leadership to guide a team of engineers through a complex project. The developer who can only write code is in a precarious position. The developer who can also lead a team, communicate a vision, and mentor junior engineers is more valuable than ever.

This pattern is not unique to tech. Consider the digital marketer who built a career on mastering the specific tricks of Google's search algorithm. For years, they were a valuable asset. But when the algorithm changes, or when an AI can generate perfectly optimized content in seconds, their value plummets. The marketer who, on the other hand, understands the timeless principles of human psychology, brand storytelling, and market positioning can use any new tool to achieve their goals. Their value is not tied to the trick; it is tied to the strategy.

This is the trap of tech tricks. By over-indexing on a narrow, technical skill, you are inadvertently making yourself more automatable. You are competing directly with the machine on its home turf of speed and efficiency, a competition you cannot win in the long run.

The strategic escape from this trap is to invert your focus. Instead of building your career on a foundation of fleeting technical skills, you must build it on a foundation of durable human skills and then use technology as a flexible, adaptable layer on top. The data on this is unequivocal. A 2024 LinkedIn report found that 9 in 10 executives now agree that soft skills, or as we should call them, durable human skills, are more important than ever.[149] Similarly, analysts at the research firm Gartner have identified a "human-centric" future of work, where the most successful professionals will be those who can combine their human judgment and expertise with the power of AI.[150]

This is because the durable skills of the C.H.A.T. model, Creativity, Humanity, Adaptability, and Thinking, are tool-agnostic. Your ability to think critically does not become obsolete when a new AI model is released. Your capacity for empathy does not have a shrinking half-life. Your skill in communicating a complex idea in a simple, compelling way is just as valuable in an age of AI as it was in an age of print. These are the bedrock skills that allow you to learn and adapt to any new technology that comes along. A useful metaphor is to think of these durable skills as your professional operating system, and the specific technical tools as the apps. Learning a new AI tool is like installing a new app on your phone. It is useful, but the app is worthless without the powerful operating system that runs it. The power user focuses on constantly upgrading their OS, knowing that this will allow them to run any app the future throws at them.

The long game, therefore, is a deliberate and strategic bet on your own humanity. It is the recognition that in a world where the "how" of many tasks is being automated, your greatest value lies in the "why" and the "who." The "why" is your ability to provide strategic direction, to ask the right questions, to understand the business context, and to make wise judgments in the face of ambiguity. The "who" is your ability to connect with other humans, to lead, to mentor, to persuade, and to build relationships of trust. These are the domains where machines are weakest and where our human edge is most pronounced. The product manager in our opening story understood this instinctively. She did not try to become a better data analyst than the AI. She chose to become a better strategist, a better mentor, and a better storyteller. She chose to play the long game.

Section 2: The "AI Translator": Your New Role

The strategic response to the trap of tech tricks is not to abandon technology, but to ascend to a new role in relation to it. The most resilient and valuable professionals of the future will not be the best operators of a single AI tool; they will be the best orchestrators of human-AI systems. They will be the indispensable guides, curators, and strategists who can bridge the vast gap between the raw, computational power of the machine and the complex, nuanced needs of the business. This is the new, emergent role of the "AI Translator."

This is not necessarily a formal job title, although in some cases it is becoming one. It is a new mode of operating, a new way of creating value. The AI Translator is the professional who understands enough about the technology to see its potential, but whose primary expertise lies in their own domain, in marketing, in finance, in law, in healthcare. They are the human API (Application Programming Interface), the critical connection point that allows the power of the AI to be intelligently applied to real-world problems. They are the ones who can take a vague business goal, like "improve customer satisfaction," and translate it into a series of specific, answerable questions that an AI can help solve.

The most powerful metaphor for this new partnership is the concept of the "centaur." In the late 1990s, after his historic defeat by IBM's Deep Blue supercomputer, the chess grandmaster Garry Kasparov did not retreat from technology. Instead, he pioneered a new form of the game called "Advanced Chess," where human players could team up with computer partners. The results were astonishing. The centaur teams, combining human intuition, creativity, and strategic oversight with the computer's brute-force calculative power, could consistently beat any human grandmaster or any computer playing alone. Kasparov's insight was profound: the goal was not to compete with the machine, but to collaborate with it. He argued that our "humanity is a strength, not a weakness" in this partnership.[147] The human provides the strategic vision, the creative leaps, and the ability to adapt to novel situations. The AI provides the flawless memory, the tireless analysis of millions of possibilities, and the execution of complex calculations. The human understands the why; the AI executes the what.

This centaur model is the blueprint for the future of professional work. We are already seeing how traditional roles are evolving to fit this new paradigm, transforming from roles of pure execution to roles of strategic orchestration.

Consider the role of a corporate librarian or a research analyst. In the past, their value was in their ability to find and retrieve information. Today, an AI can perform that task with superhuman speed. The role is not disappearing; it is evolving. The modern information professional is becoming an "information curator" or a "knowledge strategist." They use AI as a powerful search and synthesis engine, but their unique value lies in the human skills they apply to the AI's output. They use their critical thinking to evaluate the quality and bias of the sources the AI provides. They use their deep domain expertise to synthesize the information into a coherent strategic insight. And they use their communication skills to present that insight in a compelling way to decision-makers. They are the centaur, combining their human wisdom with the AI's vast knowledge base to deliver a product that is far more valuable than raw information. They are the trusted guardian against the AI's potential for hallucination, the human who verifies and validates, ensuring that the organization is making decisions based on truth, not on plausible-sounding fiction.

The same transformation is happening to the role of the project manager. For decades, a significant portion of a project manager's time was consumed by administrative drudgery: tracking tasks, updating timelines, generating status reports, and nagging team members for updates. AI is rapidly automating these functions. The project manager's role is evolving away from being the "chief administrator" and toward being the "chief orchestrator." With the AI handling the mechanical aspects of project tracking, the human project manager is freed to focus on the deeply human and far more valuable work of leadership: motivating the team, resolving the inevitable interpersonal conflicts that arise in any complex project, navigating the complex web of stakeholder politics, and making the difficult strategic trade-offs when a project goes off course. The AI can manage the Gantt chart; only a human can manage the team's morale. The AI can flag a missed deadline; only a human can sit down with a struggling team member, understand the root cause of the delay, and offer the support and resources needed to get back on track.

This model of human-AI collaboration is not just a more effective way to work; it is what professionals themselves instinctively desire. The Stanford HAI study found that the most preferred form of collaboration between humans and AI was an "equal partnership," a state where the human retains a high degree of agency and works alongside the AI as a collaborator.[148] The role of the AI Translator is the perfect embodiment of this desired partnership. It is a role that keeps the human in control, providing the strategic direction and the ethical oversight, while leveraging the machine as a powerful tool for execution.

Forward-thinking companies are beginning to recognize the immense value of this role and are creating formal pathways to cultivate it. The airline Virgin Atlantic's "AI Champion" apprenticeship is a prime example. By taking employees from non-technical departments like Finance and Communications and training them to become internal AI experts, the company is deliberately building a network of AI Translators.[149] These champions are not expected to become data scientists. They are expected to remain experts in their own fields, but to be armed with a new set of tools that allows them to see and seize opportunities for AI-driven innovation from the ground up. This is a powerful model for any organization. It recognizes that the best ideas for how to apply AI will not come from a centralized IT department, but from the people who are closest to the work itself.

Section 3: Playing the Long Game with Purpose and Wisdom

The final and most profound strategy for building a career that lasts is to anchor it in the one thing that artificial intelligence will never possess: a sense of purpose. The long game is not about accumulating the most tech tricks or even about becoming the most effective AI Translator. It is about building a professional life that is grounded in your core values and dedicated to making a meaningful impact. This is the ultimate source of resilience, the internal compass that will guide you through the inevitable twists and turns of a long and evolving career.

Playing the long game means deliberately cultivating and deploying your human "superpowers," the capabilities that are at the very heart of the C.H.A.T. model. These are the skills that do not just add value to a business; they add meaning to a life.

The first of these superpowers is storytelling. In a world overflowing with data, facts, and information, the ability to weave that raw material into a compelling narrative is more valuable than ever. An AI can generate a list of bullet points, but it cannot tell a story that moves a team to action, that persuades a skeptical client, or that builds a brand that people love. Storytelling is a deeply human art that connects with our emotions, our values, and our shared sense of identity.

The leader who can tell a clear and inspiring story about the future will always be more effective than the one who can only present a spreadsheet. The marketer who can craft a narrative that resonates with a customer's deepest aspirations will always outsell the one who can only list a product's features. An AI can generate a report showing that customer churn has increased by 5 percent. A human storyteller can take that same data and frame it as a narrative: "We are losing 5 percent of our customers because we have broken a promise to them. Here is the story of one of those customers, and here is my plan for how we can win back their trust." The data provides the what; the story provides the why and the so what.

The second superpower is mentorship. An AI can be a phenomenal tutor, providing instant access to information and personalized learning paths. But it cannot be a mentor. A mentor does not just transfer knowledge; they share wisdom. They provide encouragement in moments of doubt, offer candid feedback based on years of lived experience, and use their own social capital to open doors for their mentees. Mentorship is a relationship, a human-to-human connection built on trust, generosity, and a genuine desire to see another person succeed.

An AI cannot share a story of a time it failed and what it learned from the experience. It cannot offer a word of encouragement based on a shared understanding of the challenges of a particular corporate culture. In a world where entry-level roles are being automated, the role of the human mentor who can guide the next generation of talent becomes even more vital. By choosing to be a mentor, you are not only making a profound impact on someone else's career; you are also engaging in one of the most powerful forms of learning and solidifying your own expertise.

The third and most important superpower is ethical judgment. This is the ultimate human advantage, the one area where we must never cede control to the machine. As one essay on the topic of AI and experience noted, "In a landscape where AI can generate code and automate tasks, companies need human judgment more than ever... experience and wisdom are a strategic advantage that AI can't replicate."[150] An AI can be programmed to follow a set of rules, but it cannot navigate the gray areas of a complex ethical dilemma. It can optimize for a given objective, but it cannot decide if the objective itself is a worthy one.

This is where your accumulated wisdom becomes your most valuable asset. As a thought leader on the subject of leadership wrote, "Remember that AI is a tool, but you are the heart. Empathy, compassion, intuition, humor, vulnerability: these are the gifts only human leaders can bring. AI can suggest what is wise; only you can choose what is right. AI can surface information; only you can touch a soul. Wisdom lives not just in answers, but in how those answers are shared and lived."[151]

Playing the long game means deliberately seeking out opportunities to exercise these superpowers. It means choosing to be the storyteller who translates data into meaning, the mentor who invests in the growth of others, and the ethical steward who ensures that technology is used in service of our shared human values. These are the roles that will never be automated. They are the roles that will define the most resilient, the most respected, and the most fulfilled professionals of the 21st century.

Conclusion

The journey through this book began with a question born of anxiety: Is AI coming for my job? We have traveled from the front lines of disruption, hearing the stories of those whose careers have been upended, to the boardrooms where the future of work is being debated. We have explored the psychological landscape of this new era, the technical realities of the tools at our disposal, and the timeless value of our own humanity. The path forward, I hope you now see, is not a retreat from technology, but a strategic and wholehearted embrace of what makes us human.

The core message of this book is that you have a choice. You can view the rise of artificial intelligence as a threat that renders you obsolete, or you can see it as the most powerful tool ever created for your own liberation and advancement. The future-proof professional is not the one who can compete with the machine at its own game of speed and data processing. It is the one who chooses to play a different game altogether.

This is the long game. It is a career strategy built on three foundational pillars. First, you must double down on your Human Edge, deliberately cultivating the durable skills of Creativity, Humanity, Adaptability, and Thinking that no algorithm can replicate. Second, you must become an AI Translator, the indispensable human who can orchestrate technology, providing the context, strategy, and ethical judgment that the machine will always lack. Finally, you must anchor your professional life in a sense of purpose, leveraging your unique human superpowers of storytelling, mentorship, and wisdom to create a career that is not just resilient, but also deeply meaningful.

You now have the frameworks, the strategies, and the mental models needed to build a career that does not just survive, but thrives in the age of AI. You have a plan for adapting faster, staying human, and using AI better. The future is no longer something that is happening to you; it is something you are ready to build. The anxiety of the unknown can now be replaced by the excitement of the possible. The rest of the journey is yours. The Bonus Toolkit that follows is the first step, a collection of practical resources to help you put these principles into action today.

PART V: BONUS TOOLKIT: CAREER SURVIVAL RESOURCES

Introduction

The strategies and frameworks in this book are designed to give you a clear path forward, a new map for a new and unfamiliar landscape. You have navigated the great debate, discovered your Human Edge, and explored the playbooks for every stage of your career. Now, the journey shifts from observation to participation. This toolkit is where you take your first steps on that path. It is the bridge from understanding to action, the point where the theory of a future-proof career becomes the practice of building one.

The resources that follow are not just a collection of useful links; they are a curated set of tools designed to help you build the exact kind of professional life that workers are now demanding in the age of AI. This is not about chasing fleeting trends; it is about aligning your career with fundamental human needs in a technological age. A groundbreaking 2024 study from Stanford's Human-Centered AI Institute, "What Workers Really Want from Artificial Intelligence," provides a clear blueprint of the ideal human-AI partnership. It found that professionals overwhelmingly want to automate tedious work, use AI to accelerate their learning, and protect the creative, strategic, and interpersonal parts of their jobs that they find most meaningful.[152] This toolkit is your practical guide to achieving all three of those goals, transforming your relationship with AI from a source of anxiety into a source of agency.

Think of this section as your personal lab, a safe and structured environment for experimentation. Here, you can test your assumptions, build new skills, and create tangible proof of your capabilities without the high stakes of a live work project. The tools are organized to follow a logical progression, moving from the internal work of self-awareness and foundational learning to the external work of building your portfolio and mastering the art of the prompt. This is your opportunity to put the principles of this book into practice, one tool at a time, and to begin the deliberate, empowering work of constructing your own future.

Section 1: Self-Assessments: Know Thyself

The journey to a future-proof career begins not with a frantic search for a new job or a hasty enrollment in an online course, but with a quiet and honest act of self-reflection. Before you can design your future, you must first understand your present. Self-awareness is the foundational skill upon which all the other strategies in this book are built. You cannot know where to go if you do not have a clear and accurate map of where you are. The tools in this section are designed to help you create that map. They are a structured guide to diagnosing your risks, identifying your strengths, and gaining the clarity you need to make your next move a strategic one, not a panicked one.

The Stanford HAI study revealed a crucial tension that every professional must navigate: the desire to automate the drudgery of work while protecting the meaningful tasks that provide a sense of purpose and fulfillment.[153] The tools that follow will help you apply this powerful insight directly to your own role. The AI Task Audit will help you deconstruct your job to see where that line between drudgery and meaning lies for you. The Human Edge Scorecard will help you inventory the very skills that make your meaningful work so valuable. And the final set of resources will help you measure your resilience and build a concrete plan to bridge the gap between the professional you are today and the one you want to become.

Tool 1: The AI Task Audit

This first tool is a powerful, hands-on exercise that uses an AI to help you audit your own work. It is a multi-step prompt designed to be used with a generative AI tool like ChatGPT. It will walk you through a process of inventorying your daily tasks and then provide a detailed analysis, separating the work that is a prime candidate for automation from the work that requires your unique human skills. This is the practical application of the "Creep Risk" Audit we discussed in Chapter 9, supercharged with the analytical power of AI itself.

How to Use This Tool:
Simply copy the entire prompt below and paste it into your AI chat interface of choice. The AI, acting as your personal productivity strategist, will then guide you through the process one step at a time. Be thoughtful and honest in your responses; the more accurate your input, the more valuable the output will be.

Prompt: The AI Task & Human Edge Audit
Persona: You are "Aura," an expert AI career and productivity strategist. Your goal is to help me audit my daily and weekly tasks to identify opportunities for automation and to pinpoint where my unique human skills create the most value.
Instructions:

Step 1: Task Collection

First, ask me to list 10-20 of my most common daily or weekly work tasks. Wait for my response before proceeding.

Step 2: Task Categorization

Once I provide the list, you will ask me to rate each task on two scales from 1 to 5:

1. **Effort to Complete**: (1 = Low effort, 5 = High effort)
2. **Energy & Enjoyment**: (1 = Draining, 5 = Energizing)

   Wait for my response before proceeding.

Step 3: AI Analysis (Four Quadrants)

After I provide the ratings, analyze my list and categorize the tasks into four quadrants. Present this in a simple table:

- **Automate Zone (Low Energy, High Effort)**: Tasks that are prime candidates for automation.
- **Delegate Zone (Low Energy, Low Effort)**: Tasks that could be delegated or streamlined.
- **Thrive Zone (High Energy, High Effort)**: Core responsibilities where I feel engaged and effective.
- **Flow Zone (High Energy, Low Effort)**: Tasks that are easy and enjoyable for me.

Step 4: Human Edge vs. Automation Analysis

Next, provide a deeper analysis based on the

"Human Edge" framework. For each task, assess whether it is primarily:

- **Automatable**: Repetitive, rule-based, or data-processing-heavy.
- **Human-Centric:** Requiring skills that AI struggles to replicate, such as Empathy, Presence, Opinion, Creativity, or Hope (the EPOCH framework).

  Explain your reasoning for each assessment in a bulleted list.

Step 5: Actionable Recommendations

Finally, provide a summary report with actionable recommendations. This should include:

- A prioritized list of tasks to consider automating or delegating.
- Suggestions for specific types of AI tools or strategies for the "Automate Zone" tasks.
- A summary of my "Human Edge" tasks and advice on how to focus more of my time and energy on them to increase my strategic value and career resilience.

This prompt is based on the EPOCH framework developed by researchers at MIT, which identifies the core human-centric capabilities as Empathy, Presence, Opinion, Creativity, and Hope.[154] By the end of this exercise, you will have a personalized, data-driven report that provides a clear and actionable roadmap for redesigning your role. The tasks in your "Automate Zone" are your immediate targets for applying the power user techniques we will explore later in this toolkit. The tasks in your "Thrive Zone" and "Flow Zone" are the core of your Human Edge, the areas where you should be investing the majority of your professional development energy.

Tool 2: The Human Edge Scorecard

The AI Task Audit helps you identify which of your tasks are most human-centric. This next tool, the Human Edge Scorecard, is designed to help you assess how strong you are in the four core capabilities of the C.H.A.T. model. This is not a scientifically validated psychological test, but a structured self-reflection exercise. Its purpose is to help you move from a vague sense of your strengths to a more specific and quantified understanding of your unique Human Edge.

How to Use This Tool:

For each of the four pillars below, read the description and then rate yourself on a scale of 1 to 5 for each of the corresponding statements (1 = Rarely, 5 = Consistently).

C: Creativity

This is your ability to generate novel ideas, to connect disparate concepts, and to approach problems from unconventional angles.

1. I actively seek out new information and experiences to fuel my creative thinking. (1-5)
2. When faced with a problem, I generate multiple possible solutions before choosing one. (1-5)
3. I am comfortable with ambiguity and enjoy the process of brainstorming without a clear, immediate outcome. (1-5)

4. I have a track record of proposing and implementing new ideas or process improvements in my work. (1-5)
5. I can effectively communicate a new or complex idea to others in a compelling way. (1-5)
   Total Creativity Score: ____ / 25

H: Humanity

This is your capacity for empathy, ethical judgment, and building deep, trust-based relationships. It is your ability to connect with, influence, and mentor other people.

1. I am skilled at listening to others and understanding their perspectives, even when I disagree. (1-5)
2. My colleagues would describe me as a trustworthy and reliable team member. (1-5)
3. I am comfortable navigating difficult interpersonal situations and helping to resolve conflicts. (1-5)
4. I actively look for opportunities to mentor or support the growth of my colleagues. (1-5)
5. When making decisions, I consciously consider the ethical implications and the impact on other people. (1-5)
   Total Humanity Score: ____ / 25

A: Adaptability

This is your skill of learning, unlearning, and navigating change with a positive and proactive mindset. It is your psychological resilience in the face of uncertainty.

1. When faced with a setback or failure, I tend to view it as a learning opportunity rather than a final verdict. (1-5)

2. I am genuinely curious and enjoy the process of learning new skills, even when it is difficult. (1-5)
3. I can remain productive and focused even when a project's goals or requirements are unclear or changing. (1-5)
4. I proactively seek out new challenges that push me outside of my comfort zone. (1-5)
5. I am quick to experiment with new tools and technologies to see how they can improve my work. (1-5)

   Total Adaptability Score: ____ / 25

T: Thinking

This is your ability to apply critical thought, contextual understanding, and common sense to solve complex problems. It is your capacity for judgment in a world of abundant information.

1. When presented with new information, my first instinct is to question its source and look for potential biases. (1-5)
2. I can effectively deconstruct a large, complex problem into smaller, more manageable parts. (1-5)
3. I am skilled at synthesizing information from multiple sources to form a coherent and insightful point of view. (1-5)
4. I am comfortable making decisions with incomplete information, relying on my judgment and experience. (1-5)
5. I can anticipate the second- and third-order consequences of a decision. (1-5)

   Total Thinking Score: ____ / 25

After completing the scorecard, look at your total scores. The areas where you scored highest are your current superpowers, the core of your Human Edge. The areas where you scored lowest are your greatest opportunities for growth. This scorecard provides the data you need to begin building a targeted personal development plan.

Tool 3: Career Resilience and Skills-Gap Templates

The final step in the self-assessment process is to bridge the gap between your current state and your desired future. The AI Task Audit has shown you what you should be working on. The Human Edge Scorecard has shown you where your innate strengths lie. These final tools will help you measure your psychological readiness for the journey and create a concrete plan to get there.

1. Measure Your Resilience

A successful career pivot requires a high degree of psychological resilience. The "Resilience Test" from Psychology Today is a high-quality, free assessment that can provide a valuable baseline measurement of this critical attribute. The quiz is based on established psychological scales and measures key traits of resilience, such as your ability to bounce back from setbacks, regulate your emotions, maintain a positive outlook, and problem-solve effectively.[155] Taking this 20-question quiz can provide valuable insights into your current mental and emotional readiness for a period of significant professional change. The results can help you identify specific areas for development, such as building a stronger support network or practicing the self-talk reframing techniques we discussed in Chapter 15.

2. **Map Your Skills Gap**

With a clear understanding of your strengths and your destination, the final step is to create a plan to bridge the gap. A skills-gap analysis template is a simple but powerful tool for this. The professional development organization AIHR offers an excellent, free Skills Gap Analysis worksheet that you can download and use.[156] The template provides a structured format for:

- **Listing your current skills**: This is where you can input the strengths you identified in your Human Edge Scorecard.
- **Defining the skills required for your "North Star" role**: This is based on the research you did in the first step of your five-year roadmap.
- **Identifying the gap**: This is a clear, side-by-side comparison of where you are and where you need to be.
- **Creating an action plan**: For each identified skill gap, you can outline the specific learning resources you will use (such as the courses we will explore in the next section) and set a target date for completion.

By using these three tools in sequence, you can move from a state of unstructured anxiety to one of empowered clarity. You will have a deep, data-informed understanding of your current role, your innate strengths, and your psychological readiness for change, along with a concrete, actionable plan for building the skills you need to design a career that will not expire.

Section 2: Top Learning Platforms: Build Your Foundation

The journey from a casual user of AI to a confident power user begins with a single, deliberate step: building a solid foundation of knowledge. As the Stanford HAI study revealed, a primary desire among professionals is to use AI as a tool for their own learning and skill development.[157] The resources in this section are your starting blocks for that journey. AI fluency is the new core competency of the modern professional world, the new "Excel literacy" that is rapidly becoming a baseline expectation. But the landscape of online education can be a confusing and overwhelming place, filled with a dizzying array of courses, certificates, and bootcamps, all promising to make you an AI expert.

This section is a curated guide, a clear and simple map to the best starting points for the non-technical professional. The goal here is not to learn how to code machine learning models from scratch. It is to build the conceptual understanding and the strategic vocabulary you need to use AI effectively, to lead teams in an AI-integrated environment, and to make informed decisions about how this technology can and should be used in your career. The platforms and courses that follow have been selected for their quality, their accessibility, and their direct relevance to the challenges and opportunities facing the modern knowledge worker.

Platform 1: Coursera (The Accessible University)

Coursera has established itself as a global leader in online education by partnering with top universities and companies to offer a vast catalog of courses, certificates, and even full degree programs. For the professional seeking to build a foundation in AI, it is arguably the best place to start, offering a blend of academic rigor and practical, real-world application. I began my AI journey with several Coursera courses.

The platform's key advantage is its "freemium" model; most courses can be audited for free, giving you access to all the lecture materials, with an option to pay if you want to complete the assignments and earn a certificate. Once you commit to taking a course, you can pay for a single course or pay for an annual subscription of unlimited courses (Coursera Plus). Keep an eye out for discounts of up to 50% off the annual subscription.

The Gold Standard: Andrew Ng's "AI For Everyone"
If you take only one course to begin your AI learning journey, this should be it. Taught by Andrew Ng, the co-founder of Coursera, a former lead of the Google Brain project, and a globally respected pioneer in the field of artificial intelligence, "AI For Everyone" is the definitive introduction for a non-technical audience. Ng possesses a rare gift for demystifying complex topics, and this course is a masterclass in clear, conceptual explanation.

Over approximately six hours of video lectures, the course provides a comprehensive overview of the AI landscape. You will learn the difference between Artificial Intelligence, Machine Learning, and Deep Learning. You will understand what a neural network is, not through complex mathematics, but through simple, intuitive analogies. The course is built on a powerful philosophy: to effectively work with AI, you do not need to know how to build an AI, but you do need to know what an AI can and cannot do. Ng focuses on building your strategic intuition. You will learn what makes a machine learning project feasible, what kind of data is required to train a model, and how to spot opportunities for AI within your own business or industry. The course is explicitly designed for business leaders, marketing managers, product managers, and any professional who needs to be able to have an intelligent conversation about AI, even if they never write a line of code. It is the foundational language course for the new world of work.[158]

The Essential Sequel: "Generative AI for Everyone"
After the explosion of generative AI tools like ChatGPT, Andrew Ng released a follow-up course that is the perfect second step in your learning journey. "Generative AI for Everyone" focuses specifically on the technology behind the tools that are having the most immediate impact on the workplace. In about five hours of content, this course explains, in simple terms, what a large language model (LLM) is, how it works, and the common patterns of its application, from brainstorming and writing assistance to more advanced uses. It also provides a clear-eyed look at the limitations and risks of the technology, including the persistent problem of hallucination. Completing this course will give you a much deeper and more nuanced understanding of the generative AI tools you are likely already using, transforming you from a simple user into a more strategic and critical one.[159]

The Deeper Dive: IBM's "AI Foundations for Everyone"

For those who want to move beyond a single course and engage in a more comprehensive learning path, the "AI Foundations for Everyone" specialization from IBM is an excellent choice. This is a four-course series that covers the fundamentals of AI, its applications, and its ethical implications in greater depth. Because it is designed as a specialization, it offers a more structured and scaffolded learning experience. What makes the IBM program particularly valuable is its focus on hands-on, practical application, even for a non-technical audience. In one of the later courses, you will be guided through the process of building your own simple, no-code AI chatbot. This project-based approach is a powerful way to solidify your learning, moving from abstract concepts to a tangible, working product. It is a perfect illustration of the "vibe coding" mindset, allowing you to experience the process of creation without the steep learning curve of traditional programming.[160]

Platform 2: edX & University Programs (The Ivy League Connection)

Like Coursera, edX is a leading provider of massive open online courses (MOOCs), founded by Harvard University and MIT. It offers a similar range of courses from top-tier universities and is another excellent source for foundational AI knowledge.

The Public Service Masterpiece: "Elements of AI"

This course is unique. Developed by the University of Helsinki, "Elements of AI" was created as a public service, a national and now global initiative to educate the general public about artificial intelligence. It is completely free, web-based, and self-paced. The course is divided into two parts. The first, "Introduction to AI," is a philosophical and conceptual exploration of what AI is, with no complex math or programming required. The second part, "Building AI," offers a slightly more technical but still accessible introduction to the practical mechanics of creating machine learning models. The course is beautifully designed, with clear writing and interactive exercises. Its reputation and its mission-driven approach make it a highly credible and valuable starting point for any curious professional.[161] For those who prefer reading and interactive exercises over video lectures, this is an ideal choice.

Executive Education: The Next Level
For mid-career professionals in leadership positions or those aspiring to them, platforms like edX also offer a pathway to more advanced, executive-level education. Programs like MIT Sloan's "AI for Business Strategy" or the short courses offered by Harvard Business School are designed for a different purpose. They are less about the technical fundamentals and more about the strategic implications of AI for corporate governance, competitive advantage, and organizational design. While these programs represent a significant investment of time and money, they offer a powerful signal to the market and provide access to a network of peers who are grappling with the same high-level challenges.[162]

Platform 3: Specialized & Free Initiatives (The Practical and Purpose-Driven Path)

The final category of learning resources is a diverse collection of more specialized platforms and mission-driven organizations. These are excellent options for those who want to move beyond foundational knowledge and toward a specific career outcome, or for those seeking learning opportunities outside the traditional university-affiliated platforms.

For the Career Switcher: Udacity Nanodegrees
Udacity has carved out a niche in the online education market with its "Nanodegree" programs. These are intensive, project-based learning experiences designed to get you job-ready for a specific, in-demand tech role. While many nanodegrees are highly technical, programs like the "AI Product Manager" nanodegree are perfectly suited for the mid-career professional looking to pivot into a hybrid "AI + X" role. This program does not teach you to be an AI engineer; it teaches you how to lead a team of AI engineers. You will learn the entire lifecycle of an AI product, from identifying a business opportunity and scoping a project to managing the development process and bringing a product to market. The curriculum is built around a series of real-world projects that become the foundation of your professional portfolio. While nanodegrees are a significant financial investment, their project-based methodology and direct career focus make them a powerful accelerator for those who are serious about making a significant career change.[163]

For Accessible, Practical Learning: Free Initiatives
The drive to build a more AI-fluent workforce has led to the creation of a number of high-quality, free learning resources. Google's AI Essentials course is a standout in this category. It is a short, practical, and highly accessible program that focuses on the immediate, real-world application of generative AI tools. In less than five hours, you will learn the fundamentals of prompting, how to use AI for brainstorming and writing, and how to apply these tools in common business scenarios.[164]

For those who are passionate about building a more diverse and inclusive technology workforce, there are a number of mission-driven, non-profit organizations that offer free AI education. AI4ALL is a prominent example, with a focus on providing AI education to underrepresented high school students. Fast.ai is another, with a mission to make deep learning accessible to everyone through its practical, code-first courses. These organizations are not just providing technical training; they are building a more equitable future for the field of AI. Major corporations are also contributing to this effort. The AWS Generative AI Scholarship, a partnership between Amazon and Udacity, is a $12 million program providing free training and certificates to over 50,000 students from underserved and underrepresented communities, a powerful investment in building a more diverse talent pipeline.[165] For the motivated learner, these initiatives demonstrate that a lack of financial resources does not have to be a barrier to entry into the world of AI.

Section 3: Your Information Diet: Stay Current Without Burning Out

The relentless pace of change in the age of AI presents a profound paradox. On one hand, the need to stay current has never been more urgent. On the other, the sheer volume of news, research, and opinion pieces has created a state of information overload that is a direct threat to our mental health and productivity. This is not just a feeling of being busy; it is a diagnosable condition with severe consequences. Research has shown that information overload costs the U.S. economy at least $900 billion annually in lost productivity, driven by the fact that employees spend nearly a third of their workday simply searching for the information they need.[158] Constant interruptions from a high volume of information have been shown to cause an average 10-point drop in IQ.[159] The psychological toll is equally high, with 80 percent of workers reporting that information overload adds to their daily stress.[160]

To navigate this landscape, you must abandon the futile attempt to know everything and instead adopt the disciplined practice of curating a "healthy information diet." Just as a nutritional diet requires a conscious plan to consume high-quality fuel and avoid junk food, an information diet requires a deliberate strategy to consume high-signal knowledge and filter out low-value noise. This section is your guide to building that strategy. It is a curated list of the best newsletters, podcasts, and YouTube channels for staying informed without feeling overwhelmed.

Resource 1: Essential Newsletters (Your Daily Intelligence Briefing)

Newsletters are the most efficient way to get a high-level overview of the AI landscape as part of a daily routine. A well-curated newsletter does the initial work of filtering for you, delivering the most important developments directly to your inbox. The key is to be ruthless in your curation. Subscribing to one or two of the following is a strategic choice; subscribing to all of them is a recipe for the very overload you are trying to avoid.

- **The Neuron**: With over 550,000 subscribers, The Neuron has established itself as the go-to daily briefing for professionals who need to understand the business implications of AI. Its format is a masterclass in information design: a quick, scannable summary of the top AI news, a slightly deeper dive into a single major trend, and a curated list of new AI tools and how to use them. It excels at translating complex technical announcements into practical business insights. For example, when a new open-source model is released, The Neuron will not just report on its technical specifications; it will explain what this means for startups, for enterprise adoption, and for the competitive landscape. It is the perfect resource for the busy professional who needs to stay current in about five minutes a day.[161]

- **Ben's Bites:** While The Neuron focuses on business trends, Ben's Bites is laser-focused on the practical application of AI, particularly for non-technical users. With over 120,000 subscribers, its tagline is that it "helps non-technical folks build apps with AI."[162] This is the newsletter for the aspiring power user and the side-project enthusiast. It is less about the corporate strategy of the big tech companies and more about the innovative new tools emerging from the startup ecosystem. Each issue is a treasure trove of new applications, clever prompting techniques, and inspiring examples of what people are building with AI. Reading Ben's Bites is like having a very smart, very curious friend who spends their entire day scouring the internet for the coolest new AI tools and then sends you a daily summary of their findings.

- **Latent Space**: For those who want to go a level deeper and understand the thinking of the engineers and researchers who are building the technology, Latent Space is an excellent choice. Written by the tech insiders swyx & Alessio, this newsletter and its companion podcast are aimed at the "AI Engineer."[163] Do not let the title intimidate you. While some of the content is technical, it provides an invaluable inside look at the emerging trends in AI architecture, open-source models, and the ongoing debate about the future of the field. Reading Latent Space is like being a fly on the wall in a high-level Silicon Valley strategy session. It gives you a powerful sense of where the technology is heading, often months before it hits the mainstream press.

Resource 2: Must-Listen Podcasts (Learning on the Go)

Podcasts are the ideal medium for deeper, more contextual learning. They can be integrated into the otherwise unproductive moments of your day (e.g., your commute, your workout, your household chores) turning that time into a valuable learning opportunity. As with newsletters, the key is to choose a small number of high-quality shows that align with your specific learning goals.

- **Everyday AI**: Hosted by Jordan Wilson, this daily livestream and podcast is perhaps the most practical and career-focused AI show available. Its mission is to "help everyday people grow their careers with AI."[164] Wilson does an excellent job of breaking down complex topics into simple, actionable advice. The show often features interviews with professionals who are using AI in innovative ways in their own fields, providing a steady stream of real-world case studies and inspiration. The daily format is its unique strength. By making the show a part of your daily routine, you engage in a form of micro-learning that builds your knowledge base incrementally, without ever feeling overwhelming. It is the perfect companion for the professional who is focused on the immediate, practical application of AI in their daily work.

- **AI in Business:** Hosted by Daniel Faggella of the market research firm Emerj, this weekly podcast is aimed at a non-technical leadership audience. It features interviews with AI executives from major corporations, and the conversation is focused on the strategic application and return on investment of AI initiatives.[165] This is the podcast for the aspiring leader, the professional who wants to understand not just how to use AI, but how to build a business case for it. Listening to this show will equip you with the language and the frameworks to have a strategic conversation about AI with senior leadership, a vital skill for anyone looking to advance in their career.
- **The AI Daily Brief (Formerly The AI Breakdown)**: Hosted by Nathaniel Whittemore (NLW), this is a daily podcast and video that provides news and analysis on all things artificial intelligence.[166] This is my favorite way to stay up to date on the latest AI news. Whittemore excels at connecting the dots between seemingly disparate news items, providing a coherent narrative of the week's developments in the AI world.

Resource 3: Key YouTube Channels; Seeing is Believing

For many people, the most effective way to understand a new technology is to see it in action. YouTube has become an invaluable resource for visual learners, offering everything from high-level explainers to detailed, step-by-step tutorials.

- **AI Explained**: With over 300,000 subscribers, this channel has become a leading source for clear, accessible video explainers on the latest AI news and technological breakthroughs. The host does an excellent job of breaking down complex research papers and product announcements into simple, easy-to-understand terms, often using helpful visuals and analogies. If you want to understand what a new AI model like GPT-5 can actually do, this channel will likely have a video that shows you, rather than just telling you.

- **Two Minute Papers**: This channel is a masterclass in concise scientific communication. The host takes the most interesting and often mind-bending new AI research papers and explains their core concepts in a series of short, engaging videos, almost always in under five minutes. It is a thrilling and highly efficient way to get a glimpse of the cutting edge of AI research, from new developments in robotics to breakthroughs in generative video.

- **ColdFusion**: While not exclusively an AI channel, ColdFusion produces high-quality, documentary-style videos on the history and future of technology. Its deep dives into the stories of companies like OpenAI and Nvidia provide invaluable context for understanding the current AI landscape. Understanding how we got here is vital for understanding where we are going, and this channel is one of the best for that kind of historical perspective.

- **For Ethical and Societal Context**: To balance the often breathless coverage of technological progress, it is vital to engage with sources that explore the deeper ethical and societal implications of AI. The Washington Post's "Reasonable Doubts" video series and the MIT Technology Review's "In Machines We Trust" podcast are both excellent resources for this kind of critical, human-centric analysis. A true power user is not just a cheerleader for technology; they are a thoughtful and critical user who understands both its promise and its peril.

By carefully selecting one or two resources from each of these categories, you can build a personalized, balanced, and sustainable information diet. This is the first and most important step in moving from a state of reactive anxiety to one of proactive, informed confidence.

Section 4: Project Templates: Build Your Proof of Work

The previous sections of this toolkit have equipped you with the foundational knowledge and the curated information you need to understand the world of AI. This section is where you begin to shape that world. The ultimate differentiator in a crowded job market is not what you know, but what you have created. A portfolio of tangible projects is the most powerful form of proof, a direct and undeniable signal to any hiring manager that you possess the skills, the curiosity, and the initiative to create value.

This can be an intimidating prospect, especially for the non-technical professional. But as we discussed in Chapter 7, the rise of no-code platforms and the "vibe coding" mindset has democratized the act of creation. This section is your hands-on guide to getting started. It provides two distinct starter project templates, each designed to be a low-stakes, high-impact entry point into the world of building. The first will guide you through the process of building an automation engine to solve a real-world business problem. The second will introduce you to the creative and empowering world of vibe coding. These are not just technical exercises; they are your first steps toward building the portfolio that gets you hired.

Tool 1: No-Code Automation Starters

The ability to automate repetitive work is one of the most sought-after skills in the modern workplace. It is a direct demonstration of your ability to think systematically, to improve processes, and to create efficiency. This first project will guide you through the process of building a simple but powerful "Personal Productivity Engine" using a no-code platform like Zapier or Make.com. This project is a perfect starting point because it solves a real and relatable problem: managing the follow-up tasks that are generated by a busy meeting schedule.

The Project: The Automated Meeting Follow-Up Assistant

- **The Goal**: To create an automated workflow that, after a meeting concludes, uses AI to draft a professional follow-up email, ensuring that key action items are never forgotten.
- **The Tools**: A calendar app (like Google Calendar), an email client (like Gmail), and a no-code automation platform (like Zapier).
- **The Logic (A Step-by-Step Guide)**:
    1. **The Trigger**: A Keyword in Your Calendar. The workflow begins in your calendar. The trigger will be "New Event in Google Calendar." To ensure that

232

this automation only runs for specific meetings, you will add a filter. The automation will only proceed if the calendar event's title or description contains a specific keyword, such as "#followup." This simple keyword acts as your command to the system. When you are creating a calendar invitation for a meeting that you know will require a follow-up, you simply add "#followup" to the event description.

2. **The First Action**: A Strategic Delay. You do not want the follow-up email to be sent the second the meeting ends. That would feel robotic and impersonal. The first action in your workflow will be a "Delay" step. You can configure it to wait for a specific amount of time after the meeting's scheduled end time, for example, one hour. This builds a more natural and human-feeling cadence into your automation.

3. **The Second Action**: The AI Brain. This is where the intelligence comes in. The next action will be a connection to an AI model, such as ChatGPT or Claude, which are integrated directly into platforms like Zapier. You will craft a detailed prompt that provides the AI with the context it needs to draft a high-quality email. Your prompt can even pull in dynamic information from the calendar event itself. It might look something like this:
   - **Persona:** "Act as a highly organized and professional project manager."

233

- **Task**: "A meeting has just concluded. Your task is to draft a polite and professional follow-up email to the attendees."
- **Context**: "The title of the meeting was: [Insert Meeting Title from Calendar]. The attendees were: [Insert Attendees from Calendar]. The purpose of the meeting was to discuss the next steps for this project."
- **Format**: "The email should have three parts: 1) A brief thank you to the attendees for their time and participation. 2) A concise, one-sentence summary of the meeting's primary goal. 3) A clear call to action, prompting the team for the next steps. Please use placeholders like [Insert Key Action Items Here] and [Your Name] so I can easily customize the final draft."

4. **The Final Action:** Creating the Draft. The final step is to take the email that the AI has generated and do something with it. The action will be "Create Draft in Gmail." You will configure this step to take the output from the AI step and use it to create a new, unsent draft in your Gmail account, automatically addressed to the meeting attendees.

- **The Result**: One hour after your meeting ends, a perfectly formatted, professionally written draft of a follow-up email will be waiting in your Gmail drafts folder. All you need to do is fill in the specific action items that were discussed, give it a final proofread, and click send.

This simple project, which can be built in under an hour with no code, is a powerful piece of proof of work. It demonstrates to a potential employer that you possess a number of high-value skills. It shows that you are a systems thinker, capable of deconstructing a process and redesigning it for efficiency. It shows that you are proactive, actively looking for ways to improve your own productivity rather than waiting to be told what to do. And it demonstrates a sophisticated level of AI fluency, showing that you can do more than just ask an AI simple questions; you can integrate it into a complex, multi-step workflow to achieve a specific business outcome.

Tool 2: Open-Source Frameworks & Repositories

The first project focused on automating an existing process. This second project is about creating something entirely new. It is your entry point into the world of "vibe coding," the conversational, AI-assisted style of software development that is lowering the barrier to creation for everyone. For this, we will use Replit, an all-in-one, browser-based coding environment that is designed for this new, collaborative way of working. We will also explore GitHub, which is not just a place for professional developers to store their code, but a vast public library of ideas, templates, and inspiration that you can use for your own projects.

The Project: The Generative Art Sandbox
- **The Goal**: To create a unique piece of generative visual art by engaging in a conversational, iterative process with an AI assistant.
- **The Tools**: The Replit platform and its integrated AI assistant.

- **The Logic (A Step-by-Step Guide):**
    1. **Step 1:** Fork the Template. Your journey begins on Replit. You will start with a pre-built template called "p5.js Generative Art." This template provides a simple, working piece of code that generates a swirling, colorful animation. The first step is to "fork" or "remix" this template, which simply means creating your own personal, editable copy of the project in your Replit account.
    2. **Step 2:** Run and Observe. Once you have your own copy, the first thing to do is click the large "Run" button at the top of the screen. In the preview window, you will see the initial animation. This is your baseline, your starting block.
    3. **Step 3:** Initiate a "Vibe Coding" Session. Now, the creative part begins. In the Replit interface, you will open the AI assistant chat pane. This is your co-pilot. You will start a conversation with it, not by writing code, but by describing a creative vision in plain English. Your first prompt could be something like: "This is a great start, but I want the vibe to be more like a calm, rainy night. Can you change the color palette to blues and purples?"
    4. **Step 4:** Iterate and Refine. The AI will analyze your request and suggest changes to the code. It will show you the exact lines it wants to modify. You do not need to understand the code; you just need to approve the change. You will click "Apply," and you will see the live preview instantly update to reflect your new color scheme. This is the magic of

236

the tight feedback loop. From here, you continue the conversation, layering on new instructions and refining the artwork with each prompt. Your conversation might look like this:

- You: "Now, can you make the lines fall downwards like raindrops instead of swirling?"
- AI: Suggests code changes.
- You: Apply changes. "Perfect. Now, can you add a new element: small, white dots that sparkle and disappear randomly, like stars reflecting in a puddle?"
- AI: Suggests more code changes.
- You: Apply changes. "That's too many stars. Can you reduce the number of them by about half?"

- This process of iterative, conversational refinement is the core experience of vibe coding. You are acting as the creative director, guiding your AI assistant to bring your vision to life.
- **The Result:** At the end of a 30-minute session, you will have a unique piece of digital art that you created. It is a tangible, visual artifact of your creative process.

This project is a powerful addition to your portfolio because it demonstrates a different set of modern skills. It shows that you are creative and have a unique artistic vision. It shows that you are adaptable and not afraid to experiment with cutting-edge, unfamiliar tools. And it demonstrates a modern, collaborative approach to working with AI, treating it as a creative partner rather than just a simple tool.

Inspiration Hubs for Your Next Project

Once you have completed these starter projects, you will likely be hungry for more. The open-source community is a vast and generous source of inspiration. The Awesome AI Agents repository on GitHub is a curated list of hundreds of more advanced AI agent projects.[168] While many are highly technical, browsing the list can give you a powerful sense of what is possible. The Awesome ChatGPT Prompts repository is another invaluable resource, a massive, community-curated library of prompts for almost any task imaginable.[169] You can use these prompts as the building blocks for your own, more sophisticated automation engines. These repositories are your library, your sandbox, and your window into the future of what you can build.

Section 5: ChatGPT Prompt Packs: Your Career Co-Pilot

A powerful tool is only as effective as the person wielding it. In the world of generative AI, the interface between human intent and machine execution is the prompt. A vague, poorly constructed prompt will yield a generic, unhelpful response. A well-engineered prompt, on the other hand, can unlock the full potential of the AI, transforming it from a simple chatbot into a powerful, specialized co-pilot for your career. The challenge is that learning to write these sophisticated prompts takes time and practice.

This section is your shortcut. It is a curated arsenal of the best pre-built prompt packs and libraries, created by career experts and generous power users. These are not just simple lists of questions; they are thoughtfully designed, battle-tested templates that can help you automate and elevate the most challenging parts of your career navigation, from writing a standout resume to preparing for a high-stakes interview. Think of these resources as a downloadable upgrade for your AI assistant, instantly equipping it with the expertise you need to get ahead. By leveraging the work of others, you can save hundreds of hours of trial and error and begin operating at a power-user level from day one.

Resource 1: Top Gumroad & Notion Libraries

The creator economy has produced a wealth of high-quality, specialized resources for professionals. Platforms like Gumroad and Notion have become hubs for experts to share their knowledge in the form of digital products, often for free or at a very low cost. The following prompt packs are among the best and most reputable for career development.

- **For the All-in-One Job Seeker**: Jeff Su's "ChatGPT Prompts for Job Search"
  If you are looking for a single, comprehensive resource to guide you through the entire job search process, this is the place to start. Created by Jeff Su, a popular career and productivity content creator, this free Gumroad pack is a masterclass in practical application. It contains over 130 meticulously crafted prompts that cover every stage of the job hunt, from initial networking and resume writing to interview preparation and salary negotiation. The prompts are organized logically, providing a step-by-step guide. For example, there are prompts to help you tailor your resume to a specific job description, to draft compelling cover letters, to generate insightful questions to ask your interviewer, and to write professional

follow-up emails. What makes this resource particularly valuable is that it is continuously updated with the latest prompt engineering techniques, making it a living document that evolves with the technology.[170]

- **For the Strategic Applicant**: Jan Tegze's "Ultimate Guide to ChatGPT for Job Seekers"
  This resource, from the veteran recruiter and author Jan Tegze, is more than just a list of prompts; it is a 63-page strategic guide to using AI to create applications that stand out. Offered as a free eBook on Gumroad, it provides 42 curated prompts, but its real value lies in the expert context that surrounds them. Tegze does not just give you a prompt to write a resume; he explains the underlying principles of what makes a resume effective in the modern hiring landscape and then shows you how to use AI to achieve that result. It is a perfect blend of timeless recruiting wisdom and cutting-edge technological tactics. This guide is ideal for the professional who wants to understand not just the "how" of using AI, but the "why" behind a successful application.[171]

- **For the Advanced Prompt Engineer**: Hatim Rijal's "Mastering ChatGPT for Job Search"
  For those who want to move beyond simple copy-and-paste and learn a more structured methodology, this paid Gumroad guide offers a more advanced framework. Rijal introduces his proprietary "TCEPFT" method, a structured approach to prompt engineering that helps you provide the AI with the precise context it needs to generate highly personalized and effective content. This resource is for the job seeker who wants to

develop a deeper, more systematic skill in prompt design, a skill that is transferable to any professional task.[172]

- **For the Lifelong Learner**: Ignacio Velasquez's "2,500+ ChatGPT Prompt Templates"
This resource, a massive and meticulously organized Notion library, is a testament to the power of community curation. Created by Ignacio Velasquez, this collection is not limited to the job search; it is a comprehensive library of prompts for virtually every aspect of professional and personal productivity. It contains thousands of templates for tasks ranging from marketing and sales to project management and personal development. For the professional who is committed to integrating AI into every aspect of their work, this library is an invaluable, ever-growing resource that can serve as a "second brain" for your prompting efforts.[173]

Resource 2: How to Engineer a Better Prompt

While prompt packs are a fantastic starting point, the ultimate goal is to learn how to engineer your own effective prompts from scratch. This is the skill that truly separates the casual user from the power user. A well-engineered prompt is not a simple question; it is a detailed and specific set of instructions that guides the AI toward the precise output you need. The best way to learn this is to understand the core principles that make a prompt effective. While there are many complex frameworks, most of them are built on a few simple, powerful ideas.

1. Assign a Persona

The first and most important principle is to tell the AI who it should be. A large language model has been trained on a vast and diverse range of text, and it has the ability to adopt different voices, tones, and areas of expertise. By assigning a persona, you are constraining the AI's vast knowledge to the specific domain that is relevant to your task. This dramatically improves the quality and relevance of the response.

- **Vague Prompt:** "Help me prepare for my job interview."
- **Persona-Driven Prompt**: "Act as a senior hiring manager at a top-tier consulting firm. You have 20 years of experience hiring for strategy roles. I am a candidate interviewing for a Senior Consultant position. Ask me five tough, behavioral interview questions that you would ask a real candidate for this role."

The second prompt is infinitely more powerful because it transforms the AI from a generic chatbot into a specialized interview coach.

2. Provide Context

An AI is not a mind reader. It only knows what you tell it. The quality of its output is directly proportional to the quality and quantity of the context you provide. Think of yourself as a manager giving a project brief to a new assistant. The more background information, data, and examples you provide, the better the final result will be.

- **Low-Context Prompt**: "Write a cover letter for a marketing manager job."
- **High-Context Prompt**: "Act as a professional career coach. Your task is to write a compelling and personalized cover letter for me. I am applying for the Marketing Manager position at Company X. Here is the full job description: [Paste Job Description]. And here is my full resume: [Paste Resume]. The cover letter should be no

more than 300 words, and it should highlight how my experience in leading the successful 'Project Phoenix' campaign directly aligns with their requirement for someone with experience in product launches. The tone should be professional but enthusiastic."

The second prompt will produce a result that is 90 percent of the way to a finished product, because you have given the AI all the raw materials it needs to do the job.

3. Ask for a Specific Format

Without specific instructions, an AI will often deliver its response in a dense, unstructured block of text. To make the output immediately usable, you must tell the AI exactly how you want the information to be formatted.

- **Unformatted Prompt**: "What are the pros and cons of a portfolio career?"
- **Formatted Prompt**: "Analyze the pros and cons of a portfolio career for a mid-career professional. Present your analysis in a two-column table. The first column should be labeled 'Advantages' and the second 'Disadvantages.' Under each heading, provide at least five distinct points, each with a one-sentence explanation."

The second prompt gives you a clean, organized, and immediately useful piece of content that you can drop into a presentation or use as the outline for a blog post.

By consistently applying these three principles, Persona, Context, and Format, you can dramatically elevate the quality of your interactions with any AI. These are the foundational skills of the modern power user, the techniques that allow you to transform a generic tool into a personalized, high-performance co-pilot for your career.

Conclusion (Final Word for the Book)

The journey we began together started with a sense of anxiety, with the stories of professionals whose careers were disrupted by a force that seemed beyond their control. The question that hung in the air was one of vulnerability: What is going to happen to me? After navigating the great debate, exploring your Human Edge, and assembling a playbook of modern career strategies, I hope you are now asking a different and far more powerful question: What will I build next?

The end of this book is not a finish line; it is a starting line. The resources in this toolkit are not trophies to be collected; they are tools to be wielded. The knowledge you have gained is not meant to be a passive shield against the future; it is meant to be an active and offensive weapon for shaping it. The central message of this book is that the age of AI does not have to be an age of obsolescence. It can be an age of empowerment, but only for those who choose to participate in their own evolution.

The future of work is not a distant, predetermined event that will one day arrive on our doorstep. It is being built today, in a million small decisions made by professionals just like you. It is built when a manager chooses to use AI to free her team from drudgery rather than to simply cut costs. It is built when a recent graduate decides to create a portfolio project instead of just polishing his resume. It is built when a mid-career professional has the courage to start a five-year reinvention plan, to become a wise beginner in a new field.

Your journey starts tomorrow morning. When you sit down at your desk, resist the urge to fall back into the old routines. Instead, open the AI Task Audit from this toolkit and run the first analysis on your own role. Choose one newsletter from the information diet and subscribe to it. Sketch out the first, small step of a side quest that sparks your curiosity. The most powerful stance you can adopt from this day forward is one of active, intentional curiosity. Ask questions. Tinker with the tools. Share what you learn.

The machine colleague has arrived, and it is here to stay. You now understand that its intelligence is a powerful but narrow thing, a mirror reflecting the vast data of the past. Your intelligence is something different. It is creative, it is empathetic, it is adaptable, and it is wise. In a world of intelligent machines, your humanity is not a bug; it is your single greatest feature. Do not be afraid of the future. You now have the map, the compass, and the tools to build it. Go build.

Acknowledgments

To my wife, Sara, thank you for your patience with countless dinner conversations about artificial intelligence.

I would also like to acknowledge Nathaniel Whittemore's podcast, The AI Daily Brief. I get tremendous value from his daily news updates and deep dives into business use cases for AI.

Notes

Introduction

1. Charis McGowan, "'One day I overheard my boss saying: just put it in ChatGPT': the workers who lost their jobs to AI," The Guardian, May 31, 2025.
2. McGowan, "'One day I overheard my boss saying.'"
3. McGowan, "'One day I overheard my boss saying.'"
4. McGowan, "'One day I overheard my boss saying.'"
5. Jim Farley, "Ford CEO Says AI Will Replace Half of All White-Collar Workers in U.S.," LiveMint, June 28, 2025.
6. Dario Amodei, "AI Could Wipe Out Half of All Entry-Level White-Collar Jobs — and Spike Unemployment to 10–20%," Axios, May 28, 2025.
7. Robert F. Smith, "Vista CEO Warns AI Will Eliminate 60% of Finance Jobs Among Attendees," Entrepreneur, June 5, 2025.
8. Marianne Lake, "JPMorgan to Cut 10% of Operations and Account Services Staff Due to AI," Entrepreneur, May 19, 2025.
9. Arvind Krishna, "IBM CEO Says AI Has Already Replaced Hundreds of Human Resources Staff," Entrepreneur, May 13, 2025.
10. Marc Benioff, quoted in "Salesforce CEO Marc Benioff says he might not hire any new engineers this year," ITPro, January 23, 2025.
11. Tobi Lütke, internal memo to Shopify staff, April 8, 2025, as reported by Business Insider.
12. McGowan, "'One day I overheard my boss saying.'"

13. McGowan, "'One day I overheard my boss saying.'"

14. Michael Zhang, et al., "What Workers Really Want from Artificial Intelligence," Stanford University Human-Centered Artificial Intelligence (HAI), 2024.

15. GoDaddy, "Walton Goggins Revealed as Celebrity in GoDaddy Super Bowl Ad," press release, January 23, 2025.

16. GoDaddy, "Walton Goggins Revealed."

17. GoDaddy, "GoDaddy Survey: AI is a Game-Changer for Small Businesses," Spring 2025, as cited in "Small Businesses Leverage Generative AI for Growth and Productivity," AWIS, 2025.

18. Pew Research Center, survey on AI and workforce, August 2023, as cited in Caroline Castrillon, "Why Adaptability In The Workplace Is More In Demand Than Ever," Forbes, April 28, 2024.

19. "9 in 10 companies hiring want workers with ChatGPT experience," ResumeBuilder.com, April 2023.

20. PwC, "2024 AI Jobs Barometer," 2024.

21. Amala Duggirala, quoted in "An employee value proposition for the age of AI," 2025 Global Human Capital Trends, Deloitte Insights, 2025.

22. "Consulting Firm Study on AI," Harvard Business School, as cited in "Humans Embracing AI Will Surge to Unparalleled Triumph," AIMOCS, 2025.

23. McGowan, "'One day I overheard my boss saying.'"

Part I: Understand the Threat and the Opportunity

Chapter 1

24. McGowan, "'One day I overheard my boss saying.'"
25. "Klarna's AI assistant now does the work of 700 customer service agents," CNBC, February 22, 2024.
26. "How Copilot is transforming financial analysis in Excel," Microsoft 365 Blog, January 11, 2024.
27. McGowan, "'One day I overheard my boss saying.'"
28. Dr. Claudia Junker, quoted in Harvey, "2024 Year in Review," corporate report, 2024.
29. "AI Use at Work Has Nearly Doubled in Two Years," Gallup, June 16, 2025.
30. Satya Nadella, "AI Replaces 30% of Microsoft's Support Coding Roles via GitHub Copilot," FinalRound AI Blog, April 29, 2025.
31. "Introducing Magic Write: AI-powered content for Canva Docs and marketing," Canva, 2023.
32. "Khanmigo: Your AI-powered guide through learning," Khan Academy, 2023.
33. "AI for work: Write, summarize, and automate faster in Notion," Notion, 2024.

Chapter 2

34. Farley, "Ford CEO Says AI Will Replace Half of All White-Collar Workers."
35. Amodei, "AI Could Wipe Out Half of All Entry-Level White-Collar Jobs."
36. Smith, "Vista CEO Warns AI Will Eliminate 60% of Finance Jobs."

37. Krishna, "IBM CEO Says AI Has Already Replaced Hundreds of Human Resources Staff."

38. Nadella, "AI Replaces 30% of Microsoft's Support Coding Roles."

39. Lake, "JPMorgan to Cut 10% of Operations and Account Services Staff."

40. Benioff, quoted in "Salesforce CEO Marc Benioff says he might not hire any new engineers this year."

41. Lütke, internal memo to Shopify staff.

42. Jassy, internal memo to Amazon staff.

43. James Bessen, "Toil and Technology," Finance & Development, International Monetary Fund, March 2015.

44. Daron Acemoglu and David Autor, "Will Automation Take Away All Our Jobs?" TED Talk, September 2016.

45. Goldman Sachs Research, "The Potentially Large Effects of Artificial Intelligence on Economic Growth," March 2023, summarized in Forbes.

46. World Economic Forum, "The Future of Jobs Report 2023," April 2023.

47. Jensen Huang, remarks at Milken Institute Global Conference, May 2024, as reported by Economic Times Panache.

48. Karim R. Lakhani, "AI Won't Replace Humans—But Humans With AI Will Replace Humans Without AI," Harvard Business Review, August 4, 2023.

49. "AI Use at Work Has Nearly Doubled in Two Years," Gallup, June 16, 2025.

Chapter 3

50. Zhang, et al., "What Workers Really Want from Artificial Intelligence."

51. Martin Ford, quoted in "3 remarkable insights from the WEF 2023 Future of Work report," Ellis Jones, May 9, 2023.

52. Bill Gates, quoted in "Bill Gates predicts only three jobs will survive the AI takeover. Here is why," The Economic Times, March 26, 2025.

53. World Economic Forum, "The Future of Jobs Report 2023."

54. "Bill Gates predicts only three jobs will survive the AI takeover."

55. "What is Human in the Loop (HITL) and Why is it Important?" Coveo, n.d.

56. Amala Duggirala, quoted in "An employee value proposition for the age of AI," 2025 Global Human Capital Trends, Deloitte Insights, 2025.

57. Daphne S. Leger, "Adaptability is the #3 most in-demand skill," LinkedIn post, June 2025.

58. World Economic Forum, "The Future of Jobs Report 2023."

59. PwC, "2024 AI Jobs Barometer."

60. Huang, remarks at Milken Institute Global Conference.

61. Leger, "Adaptability is the #3 most in-demand skill."

Part II: Start Smart: For Early-Career Professionals

Chapter 4

62. Skilled Trades Report, as cited in various 2024 industry analyses on workforce trends.
63. Survey on tradespeople and AI, as cited in 2024 workforce and automation reports.
64. U.S. Bureau of Labor Statistics, Occupational Outlook Handbook, "Nurse Anesthetists, Nurse Midwives, and Nurse Practitioners," updated September 2023.
65. U.S. Bureau of Labor Statistics, Occupational Outlook Handbook, "Substance Abuse, Behavioral Disorder, and Mental Health Counselors," updated September 2023.
66. LinkedIn, 2025 analysis on AI skills and salary premiums, as cited in various business and technology publications.
67. World Economic Forum, "The Future of Jobs Report 2023."
68. Zhang, et al., "What Workers Really Want from Artificial Intelligence."

Chapter 5

69. Statistic on Fortune 500 companies using ATS, widely cited in HR and recruiting industry reports from sources like Jobscan and HR Technologist, 2023-2024.
70. Statistic on the average number of applications per corporate job opening, from reports by recruiting platforms like Zippia and Glassdoor, 2024.
71. Quote from a hiring manager, as cited in a 2025 recruiting industry newsletter on hiring trends.
72. Zhang, et al., "What Workers Really Want from Artificial Intelligence."

73. Survey statistic on the use of one-way video interviews, from HR technology reports by platforms like Gartner and SHRM, 2024.

Chapter 6

74. Reddit user story, as cited in various online forums and articles on AI and career development, 2024.
75. Zhang, et al., "What Workers Really Want from Artificial Intelligence."
76. Ethan Mollick, as cited in various articles on AI in education, including reports from The New York Times and The Wall Street Journal, 2023-2024.
77. David C. Banks, quoted in "New York City Public Schools End Ban on ChatGPT," The New York Times, May 18, 2023.
78. Study on junior employee productivity with AI assistants, as cited in technology and business publications, 2024.
79. Anecdote of the "grossly unqualified" intern, widely circulated in tech and AI forums, 2023.
80. Recruiter survey on in-demand skills, as cited in HR and recruiting industry reports, 2025.

Chapter 7

81. Story of Kye and CoverDoc.ai, as circulated in tech and entrepreneurship forums, 2023-2024.
82. Andrej Karpathy, definition of "vibe coding," as shared on social media and cited in tech blogs, 2023.
83. Quote from a hiring manager, as cited in a 2025 recruiting industry newsletter on hiring trends.

Chapter 8

84. Zhang, et al., "What Workers Really Want from Artificial Intelligence."
85. Zapier customer notification example, as cited in company case studies and marketing materials, 2024.

Part III: Adapt and Advance: For Mid-Career Professionals

Chapter 9

86. Reddit user story, as cited in "When do you think we'll start to see serious job displacement from AI?" Reddit, 2024.
87. Dukaan case study, as cited in "Dukaan Replaces 90% of Support Staff with AI Chatbot," Tech.co, July 11, 2023.
88. IKEA case study, as cited in "IKEA is quietly phasing out its call centre workers," Tech.co, June 1, 2023.
89. Zhang, et al., "What Workers Really Want from Artificial Intelligence."
90. Statistic on administrative/clerical task automation, from "51+ AI Statistics," Exploding Topics, updated July 2024.
91. Statistic on legal-support task automation, from "Generative AI's impact on legal jobs," TechTarget, June 2023.
92. Analysis of AI in marketing, from "How Artificial Intelligence is Shaping the Future of Marketing," Harvard Professional Development, 2024.
93. Bloomberg research, as cited in "AI Is Replacing Jobs in 2025: See Which Roles Are Disappearing," FinalRound AI, 2025.

94. Arvind Krishna, quoted in "AI will not replace people but...," People Matters, May 3, 2023.

Chapter 10

95. Amit Sharma, quoted in "Affordable, Accredited: Best Machine Learning Certification Courses Online in 2025," Medium, 2025.
96. Coursera data, as cited in "Are Professional Certificates Worth It?" Coursera Blog, 2024.
97. LinkedIn, 2024 Workplace Learning Report.
98. Marketing manager success story, as cited in "Google Career Certificates: Success Stories," Google, 2024.
99. ManpowerGroup, The New Human Age Report, 2023.
100. HR industry report, as cited in "Why AI is making soft skills a top priority for HR," HR Executive, 2024.
101. Patrick Smith, quoted in "High-Demand Human Skills In The Ongoing Age Of AI," Forbes, June 27, 2024.

Chapter 11

102. Microsoft, "How real-world businesses are transforming with AI," Microsoft Blog, April 22, 2025.
103. "How Microsoft Copilot is Streamlining Business Functions," ProserveIT, 2024.
104. Microsoft, "How real-world businesses are transforming with AI."
105. "How Microsoft Copilot is Streamlining Business Functions."
106. "How Microsoft Copilot is Streamlining Business Functions."

107.   Customer support manager, quoted in "Impact of Artificial Intelligence on the Future of Work," Indian Institute of Management Ahmedabad, 2024.

108.   Arvind Krishna, quoted in "AI will not replace people but...," People Matters, May 3, 2023.

109.   IKEA case study, as cited in "IKEA is quietly phasing out its call centre workers," Tech.co, June 1, 2023.

110.   Christos Makridis, "Play the Long Game With Human-AI Collaboration," Gallup.com, February 20, 2025.

111.   "AI in SAFe," Scaled Agile Framework, 2024.

112.   Zhang, et al., "What Workers Really Want from Artificial Intelligence."

Chapter 12

113.   "PRESS RELEASE: Virgin Atlantic Becomes First Airline to Launch AI Champion Apprenticeship with Cambridge Spark," Cambridge Spark, March 26, 2025.

114.   "How Zapier Uses AI Internally (and How You Can, Too)," Zapier, 2023.

115.   "NYU Langone Health to Hold AI 'Prompt-a-Thon' Event," NYU Langone News, August 18, 2023.

116.   LinkedIn & Microsoft, Work Trend Index: AI at Work Is Here. Now Comes the Hard Part, 2024.

Chapter 13

117.   Workday & Gallup, The State of AI at Work, 2024.

118.   KPMG, "People and AI: A Human-Centered Approach to Workplace AI Adoption," KPMG, January 20, 2025.

119.   Workday & Gallup, The State of AI at Work.

120.   "AI in SAFe," Scaled Agile Framework, 2024.

121.   Charlene Li, "How Leaders Can Use AI Ethically," Workday Blog, 2024.

122.   "AI's Take on Leadership: A New Frontier of Possibility and Reality," Three Minute Leadership (blog), May 4, 2025.

123.   HR industry report, as cited in "Why AI is making soft skills a top priority for HR," HR Executive, 2024.

Part IV: Future-Self: Build a Career That Evolves with You

Chapter 14

124.   Tanya Brno, as profiled in "Looking Ahead to 2025: How Portfolio Careers Are Replacing Traditional Jobs," Forbes, December 10, 2024.

125.   "The Great Career Reinvention, and How Workers Can Keep Up," Work Shift, May 20, 2025.

126.   World Economic Forum, "The Future of Jobs Report 2023."

127.   "Reskilling in the Age of AI," Harvard Business Review, September-October 2023.

128.   Bankrate Side Hustle Survey, as reported in Bankrate.com, February 2024.

129.   Dr. Gabby Burlacu, quoted in "Why is Gen Z embracing portfolio careers?" WFTV.com, July 22, 2025.

130.   "The Most In-Demand Skills for 2024," LinkedIn Talent Blog, February 8, 2024.

131.   Walmart, "Creating Opportunity for All American Workers," corporate news release, April 7, 2025.

132. Data on skills-first hiring, as cited in "Why a Skills-First Approach Is the Future of Hiring," Inc.com, 2024.

133. Futurist, as quoted in a Harvard Business Review article on career longevity, 2023.

134. Ikigai framework, as described in career development resources from sources like the National Association of Colleges and Employers (NACE).

135. Justin Lokitz, "How to prototype a career change, design strategy-style," California College of the Arts, 2024.

136. "Research: 64% of professionals overwhelmed by change," LinkedIn Newsroom, October 2, 2024.

Chapter 15

137. LinkedIn, "Research: 64% of professionals overwhelmed by change."

138. "Embracing Discomfort: The Path to Personal and Professional Growth," Forbes, via Camping Magazine, March 2025.

139. "7 Ways to Build Resilience in Times of Career Uncertainty," EEIHR, 2025.

140. Patti Thull, as cited in career change and reinvention articles, 2023-2024.

141. "Don't Settle, Squiggle: Why A Non-Linear Career Path Is The New Key To Success," Forbes, 2024.

142. Phoenix Insights & Ipsos, "Career Advice for Longer Lives," press release, May 18, 2023.

143. "7 Ways to Build Resilience in Times of Career Uncertainty."

144. LinkedIn, "Research: 64% of professionals overwhelmed by change."
145. "Embracing Discomfort: The Path to Personal and Professional Growth."
146. Zhang, et al., "What Workers Really Want from Artificial Intelligence."

Chapter 16

147. Garry Kasparov, as cited in discussions on human-AI collaboration and "Advanced Chess."
148. Zhang, et al., "What Workers Really Want from Artificial Intelligence."
149. "PRESS RELEASE: Virgin Atlantic Becomes First Airline to Launch AI Champion Apprenticeship with Cambridge Spark," Cambridge Spark, March 26, 2025.
150. "The Wisdom Advantage: Thriving in Tech After 50," Medium, November 8, 2023.
151. "AI's Take on Leadership: A New Frontier of Possibility and Reality," Three Minute Leadership (blog), May 4, 2025.

Part V: Bonus Toolkit: Career Survival Resources

Introduction

152. Michael Zhang et al., "What Workers Really Want from Artificial Intelligence," Stanford University Human-Centered Artificial Intelligence (HAI), 2024, https://hai.stanford.edu/news/what-workers-really-want-artificial-intelligence.

Section 1: Self-Assessments: Know Thyself

153.   Zhang, et al., "What Workers Really Want from Artificial Intelligence."

154.   "The EPOCH of AI: Human-Machine Complementarities at Work," MIT Sloan School of Management, March 17, 2025.

155.   "Resilience Test," Psychology Today, n.d.

156.   "Skills Gap Analysis Worksheet," AIHR, n.d.

Section 2: Top Learning Platforms: Build Your Foundation

157.   Zhang, et al., "What Workers Really Want from Artificial Intelligence."

158.   Coursera, AI For Everyone, online course.

159.   Coursera, Generative AI for Everyone, online course.

160.   Coursera, AI Foundations for Everyone, online course specialization.

161.   Elements of AI, online course.

162.   MIT Sloan, AI for Business Strategy, executive education course.

163.   Udacity, AI Product Manager Nanodegree, online program.

164.   Grow with Google, "AI Training – Prompting and AI Essentials."

165.   "Amazon to Provide Free AI Training to Two Million People by 2025," Innovation News Network, December 2023.

Section 3: Your Information Diet: Stay Current Without Burning Out

166.   Arjun Ken, "Living in the Era of Information Overload," Medium, March 25, 2025.

167.   Ken, "Living in the Era of Information Overload."

168.   Madeline Happold et al., "7 Ways to Cultivate a Healthy News Diet," Cascade PBS, July 26, 2025.

169.   Grant Harvey, The Neuron, newsletter.

170.   Ben Tossell, Ben's Bites, newsletter.

171.   Swyx & Alessio, Latent Space, podcast and newsletter.

172.   Jordan Wilson, Everyday AI, podcast.

173.   Daniel Faggella, AI in Business, podcast.

174.   Nathaniel Whittemore, The AI Daily Brief (Formerly The AI Breakdown), podcast.

Section 4: Project Templates: Build Your Proof of Work

175.   "Vibe Coding and AI Agents Resources," Zapier Blog.

176.   Awesome AI Agents, GitHub repository.

177.   Awesome ChatGPT Prompts, GitHub repository.

Section 5: ChatGPT Prompt Packs: Your Career Co-Pilot

178.   Jeff Su, 130+ ChatGPT Prompts for Job Seekers, Gumroad.

179.   Jan Tegze, Ultimate Guide to ChatGPT for Job Seekers, Gumroad.

180.   Hatim Rijal, Mastering ChatGPT for Job Search, Cover Letter & CV, Gumroad.

181.   Ignacio Velasquez, 2,500+ ChatGPT Prompt Templates, Notion.

Bibliography

"7 Ways to Build Resilience in Times of Career Uncertainty." EEIHR, 2025. https://eeihr.com/blog/employment-expert/7-ways-to-build-resilience-in-times-of-career-uncertainty/.

"51+ AI Statistics." Exploding Topics. Updated July 2024. https://explodingtopics.com/blog/ai-statistics.

Acemoglu, Daron, and David Autor. "Will Automation Take Away All Our Jobs?" TED Talk, September 2016. https://ideas.ted.com/will-automation-take-away-all-our-jobs/.

AIHR. "Skills Gap Analysis Worksheet." Accessed July 25, 2025. https://www.aihr.com/blog/skills-gap-analysis/.

"AI in SAFe." Scaled Agile Framework, 2024. https://www.scaledagileframework.com/ai-in-safe/.

"AI's Take on Leadership: A New Frontier of Possibility and Reality." Three Minute Leadership (blog), May 4, 2025. https://threeminuteleadership.com/2025/05/04/ais-take-on-leadership-a-new-frontier-of-possibility-and-reality/.

"AI will not replace people but..." People Matters, May 3, 2023. https://www.peoplematters.in/news/strategic-hr/ai-will-not-replace-people-but-the-person-using-ai-will-replace-you-ibm-ceo-arvind-krishna-37889.

"Amazon to Provide Free AI Training to Two Million People by 2025." Innovation News Network, December 2023. https://www.innovationnewsnetwork.com/amazon-provide-free-ai-training-two-million-people-2025/40603/.

Amodei, Dario. "AI Could Wipe Out Half of All Entry-Level White-Collar Jobs — and Spike Unemployment to 10–20%." Axios, May 28, 2025.

https://www.axios.com/2025/05/28/ai-jobs-white-collar-unemployment-anthropic.

Anecdote of the "grossly unqualified" intern. Widely circulated in tech and AI forums, 2023.

Angi Research. "Skilled Trades 2024 Report." October 2024. https://www.research.angi.com/skilled-trades-2024-report/.

"Are Professional Certificates Worth It?" Coursera Blog, 2024. https://blog.coursera.org/are-professional-certificates-worth-it/.

Awesome AI Agents. GitHub Repository. https://github.com/e2b-dev/awesome-ai-agents.

Awesome ChatGPT Prompts. GitHub Repository. https://github.com/f/awesome-chatgpt-prompts.

Bankrate. Bankrate Side Hustle Survey. February 2024. https://www.bankrate.com/personal-finance/side-hustles-survey/.

Banks, David C. Quoted in "New York City Public Schools End Ban on ChatGPT." The New York Times, May 18, 2023.

Bastian, R. "Looking Ahead to 2025: How Portfolio Careers Are Replacing Traditional Jobs." Forbes, December 10, 2024.

BCG. "Reskilling in the Age of AI." Harvard Business Review, September-October 2023.

Benioff, Marc. Quoted in "Salesforce CEO Marc Benioff says he might not hire any new engineers this year." ITPro, January 23, 2025.

Benjamin, Alex. "Why 40% of Your Job Applicants Might Not Be Real." LinkedIn, June 10, 2025. https://www.linkedin.com/pulse/why-40-your-job-applicants-might-not-real-alex-benjamin-j4vjc.

Bessen, James. "Toil and Technology." Finance & Development, International Monetary Fund, March 2015. https://www.imf.org/external/pubs/ft/fandd/2015/03/bessen.htm.

"Bill Gates predicts only three jobs will survive the AI takeover. Here is why." The Economic Times, March 26, 2025. https://economictimes.indiatimes.com/news/international/world-news/bill-gates-predicts-only-three-jobs-will-survive-the-ai-takeover-here-is-why/articleshow/108792058.cms.

Bored Panda. "'Grossly Unqualified' Intern Uses ChatGPT, Lands F500 Gigs." October 2023. https://www.boredpanda.com/unqualified-intern-chatgpt-fortune-500-internships/.

Brodnitz, D. "The Most In-Demand Skills for 2024." LinkedIn Talent Blog, February 8, 2024. https://www.linkedin.com/business/talent/blog/talent-strategy/most-in-demand-skills.

Budibase. "A Guide to AI Agents." 2024.

Burlacu, Gabby. Quoted in "Why is Gen Z embracing portfolio careers?" WFTV.com, July 22, 2025.

Business Because. "Employer Demand For AI Skills Skyrockets." GMAC Corporate Recruiter Survey, Q1 2025. https://www.businessbecause.com/news/jobs-and-careers/9335/employer-demand-ai-skills.

Business Insider. "NYC Public Schools Reverse ChatGPT Ban." May 19, 2023. https://www.businessinsider.com/nyc-public-schools-reverse-chatgpt-ban-2023-5.

Canva. "Introducing Magic Write: AI-powered content for Canva Docs and marketing." 2023.
https://www.canva.com/magic-write/.

CareerMinds. "The Future of Work: 97 Million New Jobs by 2025." Accessed July 2025.
https://www.careerminds.com/blog/future-of-work-what-jobs-will-be-in-demand.

Castrillon, Caroline. "Why Adaptability In The Workplace Is More In Demand Than Ever." Forbes, April 28, 2024.

Chief Learning Officer. "The Shrinking Half-Life of Skills." 2023.

Chowdhury, Divya. "'Great Resignation' enters third year as workers embrace AI, upskilling, PwC says." Reuters, June 25, 2024.

CNBC. "Klarna's AI assistant now does the work of 700 customer service agents." February 22, 2024.
https://www.cnbc.com/2024/02/22/klarna-ai-chatbot-doing-work-of-700-staff.html.

Coursera. AI For Everyone. Online Course.
https://www.coursera.org/learn/ai-for-everyone.

Coursera. AI Foundations for Everyone. Online Course Specialization.
https://www.coursera.org/specializations/ai-foundations-for-everyone.

Coursera. Generative AI for Everyone. Online Course.
https://www.coursera.org/learn/generative-ai-for-everyone.

Coveo. "What is Human in the Loop (HITL) and Why is it Important?" Coveo Blog, n.d.
https://www.coveo.com/blog/what-is-human-in-the-loop/.

Deloitte. "An employee value proposition for the age of AI." In 2025 Global Human Capital Trends. Deloitte Insights, 2025.

https://www.deloitte.com/us/en/insights/topics/talent/human-capital-trends/2025/why-you-need-employee-value-proposition-for-age-of-ai.html.

DigitalOcean. "12 AI Newsletters to Subscribe to in 2024." November 2023. https://www.digitalocean.com/community/tutorials/ai-newsletters-to-subscribe-to.

"Don't Settle, Squiggle: Why A Non-Linear Career Path Is The New Key To Success." Forbes, 2024.

"Dukaan Replaces 90% of Support Staff with AI Chatbot." Tech.co, July 11, 2023. https://tech.co/news/dukaan-replaces-support-staff-ai-chatbot.

edX. AI for Everyone: Master the Basics. Online Course. https://www.edx.org/course/ai-for-everyone-master-the-basics.

Elements of AI. Online Course. https://www.elementsofai.com.

Ellis Jones. "3 remarkable insights from the WEF 2023 Future of Work report." May 9, 2023. https://www.ellisjones.com.au/insights/3-remarkable-insights-from-the-wef-2023-future-of-work-report/.

"Embracing Discomfort: The Path to Personal and Professional Growth." Forbes, via Camping Magazine, March 2025.

"The EPOCH of AI: Human-Machine Complementarities at Work." MIT Sloan School of Management, March 17, 2025. https://mitsloan.mit.edu/press/new-mit-sloan-research-suggests-ai-more-likely-to-complement-not-replace-human-workers.

Ermut, Sıla. "Top 15 Predictions from Experts on AI Job Loss in 2025." AIMultiple, updated June 26, 2025. https://research.aimultiple.com/ai-job-loss/.

Faggella, Daniel. AI in Business. Podcast.

Farley, Jim. "Ford CEO Says AI Will Replace Half of All White-Collar Workers in U.S." LiveMint, June 28, 2025. https://www.livemint.com/global/ceos-start-saying-the-quiet-part-out-loud-ai-will-wipe-out-jobs-11751507282045.html.

Futurist. As quoted in a Harvard Business Review article on career longevity, 2023.

Gallup. "AI Use at Work Has Nearly Doubled in Two Years." June 16, 2025. https://www.gallup.com/workplace/691643/work-nearly-doubled-two-years.aspx.

Gartner. HR technology and hiring trends reports, 2024.

"Generative AI's impact on legal jobs." TechTarget, June 2023. https://www.techtarget.com/searchhrsoftware/news/366542151/Generative-AIs-impact-on-legal-jobs.

GoDaddy. "Walton Goggins Revealed as Celebrity in GoDaddy Super Bowl Ad." Press release, January 23, 2025. Tempe, AZ. https://aboutus.godaddy.net/newsroom/news-releases/press-release-details/2025/Walton-Goggins-Revealed-as-Celebrity-in-GoDaddy-Super-Bowl-Ad/default.aspx.

Goldman Sachs Research. "The Potentially Large Effects of Artificial Intelligence on Economic Growth." March 2023. Summarized in Forbes.

"Google Career Certificates: Success Stories." Google, 2024. https://grow.google/certificates/success-stories/.

Grow with Google. "AI Training – Prompting and AI Essentials." 2025. https://grow.google/intl/ALL/ai-training/.

Hacker, Avi. The AI Daily Brief. LinkedIn Newsletter.

Happold, Madeline, Nimra Ahmad, Sireen Abayazid, and Sophie Grossman. "7 Ways to Cultivate a Healthy News Diet." Cascade PBS. Last modified July 26, 2025. Accessed July 26, 2025.

https://www.cascadepbs.org/news/2025/03/7-ways-cultivate-healthy-news-diet/.

Harvey. "2024 Year in Review." Corporate report. 2024. https://www.harvey.ai/downloadable/year-in-review/2024/Harvey-2024-year-in-review.pdf.

Harvey, Grant. The Neuron. Newsletter. https://theneurondaily.com.

"How Artificial Intelligence is Shaping the Future of Marketing." Harvard Professional Development, 2024. https://professional.dce.harvard.edu/blog/how-artificial-intelligence-is-shaping-the-future-of-marketing/.

"How Microsoft Copilot is Streamlining Business Functions." ProserveIT, 2024. https://www.proserveit.com/blog/how-microsoft-copilot-is-streamlining-business-functions.

"How Zapier Uses AI Internally (and How You Can, Too)." Zapier, 2023. https://zapier.com/blog/ai-workflows-at-zapier.

HR Executive. "Why human skills are more vital than ever in the age of AI." August 2023. https://hrexecutive.com/why-human-skills-are-more-vital-than-ever-in-the-age-of-ai/.

Huang, Jensen. Remarks at Milken Institute Global Conference, May 2024. As reported by Economic Times Panache, "'Don't be that person who ignores this technology': Nvidia CEO warns AI will rewrite the rules of employment."

"Humans Embracing AI Will Surge to Unparalleled Triumph." AIMOCS, 2025. https://aimocs.com/humans-embracing-ai-will-surge-to-unparalleled-triumph/.

"IKEA is quietly phasing out its call centre workers." Tech.co, June 1, 2023.
https://tech.co/news/ikea-phasing-out-call-centre-workers.

Ikigai framework. As described in career development resources from sources like the National Association of Colleges and Employers (NACE).
https://www.naceweb.org/career-development/branding-and-marketing/finding-your-ikigai-a-framework-for-career-development/.

"Impact of Artificial Intelligence on the Future of Work." Indian Institute of Management Ahmedabad, 2024.
https://iima.ac.in/research-and-publication/periodicals/vikalpa/archives/volume-49-issue-1/impact-of-artificial-intelligence-on-the-future-of-work.

Inc. "Why a Skills-First Approach Is the Future of Hiring." 2024.

ISACA. "The Future of Work: A Human-Centric Approach." 2024.

Jassy, Andy. Internal memo to Amazon staff, June 17, 2025. Summarized by Business Insider.
https://www.businessinsider.com/amazon-andy-jassy-ai-agents-job-impact-workforce-2025-6.

Jobscan. Blog and industry reports on Applicant Tracking Systems, 2023-2024.

Karpathy, Andrej. Definition of "vibe coding." As shared on social media and cited in tech blogs, 2023.

Kasparov, Garry. As cited in discussions on human-AI collaboration and "Advanced Chess."

Ken, Arjun. "Living in the Era of Information Overload." Medium, March 25, 2025.

https://arjunken.medium.com/living-in-the-era-of-information-overload-fb90ba6e3577.

Khan Academy. "Khanmigo: Your AI-powered guide through learning." 2023. https://www.khanacademy.org/khan-labs.

KPMG. "People and AI: A Human-Centered Approach to Workplace AI Adoption." KPMG, January 20, 2025. https://kpmg.com/au/en/home/insights/2025/01/workplace-ai-adoption-success-insights-stories.html.

Krishna, Arvind. "IBM CEO Says AI Has Already Replaced Hundreds of Human Resources Staff." Entrepreneur, May 13, 2025. https://www.entrepreneur.com/business-news/ibm-ceo-ai-replaced-hundreds-of-human-resources-staff/491341.

kumarisakshi9595. "Affordable, Accredited: Best Machine Learning Certification Courses Online in 2025." Medium, 2025. https://medium.com/@kumarisakshi9595/affordable-accredited-best-machine-learning-certification-courses-online-in-2025-61fe74b590de.

Lake, Marianne. "JPMorgan to Cut 10% of Operations and Account Services Staff Due to AI." Entrepreneur, May 19, 2025. https://www.entrepreneur.com/business-news/jpmorgan-to-cut-headcount-in-some-divisions-due-to-ai/491864.

Lakhani, Karim R. "AI Won't Replace Humans—But Humans With AI Will Replace Humans Without AI." Harvard Business Review, August 4, 2023.

Latent Space. Podcast and Newsletter. https://www.latent.space.

LearnDataSci. "9 Best AI & Machine Learning Courses Online for 2025." 2025. https://www.learndatasci.com/best-ai-machine-learning-courses/.

Leger, Daphne S. "Adaptability is the #3 most in-demand skill." LinkedIn post, June 2025.

Li, Charlene. "How Leaders Can Use AI Ethically." Workday Blog, 2024. https://blog.workday.com/en-us/2024/how-leaders-can-use-ai-ethically.html.

LinkedIn. 2024 Workplace Learning Report. https://learning.linkedin.com/resources/workplace-learning-report.

LinkedIn. 2025 analysis on AI skills and salary premiums. As cited in various business and technology publications.

LinkedIn. "Career Resilience Quiz." Accessed July 2025.

LinkedIn. "Research: 64% of professionals overwhelmed by change." LinkedIn Newsroom, October 2, 2024. https://news.linkedin.com/2024/10/research--64--of-professionals-overwhelmed-by-change--and-how-.

LinkedIn & Microsoft. Work Trend Index: AI at Work Is Here. Now Comes the Hard Part. 2024. https://www.microsoft.com/en-us/worklab/work-trend-index/ai-at-work-is-here.

Lokitz, Justin. "How to prototype a career change, design strategy-style." California College of the Arts, 2024. https://www.cca.edu/newsroom/how-prototype-career-change-design-strategy-style/.

Lütke, Tobi. Internal memo to Shopify staff, April 8, 2025. Covered by Business Insider. https://www.businessinsider.com/shopify-hiring-freeze-ai-priority-email-ceo-tobi-lutke-2025-4.

Make.com. "AI Agents." Accessed July 2025. https://www.make.com/en/ai.

Makridis, Christos. "Play the Long Game With Human-AI Collaboration." Gallup.com, February 20, 2025. https://www.gallup.com/workplace/660572/play-long-game-human-ai-collaboration.aspx.

ManpowerGroup. The New Human Age Report. 2023. https://workforce-resources.manpowergroup.com/home/the-new-human-age.

McGowan, Charis. "'One day I overheard my boss saying: just put it in ChatGPT': the workers who lost their jobs to AI." The Guardian, May 31, 2025.

Microsoft. "How real-world businesses are transforming with AI." Microsoft Blog, April 22, 2025. https://blogs.microsoft.com/blog/2025/04/22/https-blogs-microsoft-com-blog-2024-11-12-how-real-world-businesses-are-transforming-with-ai/.

Microsoft. "How Copilot is transforming financial analysis in Excel." Microsoft 365 Blog, January 11, 2024. https://www.microsoft.com/en-us/microsoft-365/blog/2024/01/11/how-copilot-is-transforming-financial-analysis-in-excel/.

MIT Sloan. AI for Business Strategy. Executive Education Course. https://executive.mit.edu.

Mollick, Ethan. As cited in various articles on AI in education, including reports from The New York Times and The Wall Street Journal, 2023-2024.

Muck Rack. "Tanya Brno: A Portfolio Career in Action." 2024. https://muckrack.com/tanya-brno/portfolio.

Nadella, Satya. "AI Replaces 30% of Microsoft's Support Coding Roles via GitHub Copilot." FinalRound AI Blog, April 29, 2025. https://www.finalroundai.com/blog/ai-tech-layoffs-mid-2025.

Notion. "AI for work: Write, summarize, and automate faster in Notion." 2024. https://www.notion.so/product/ai.

"NYU Langone Health to Hold AI 'Prompt-a-Thon' Event." NYU Langone News, August 18, 2023. https://nyulangone.org/news/nyu-langone-health-hold-ai-prompt-thon-event.

Patti Thull. As cited in career change and reinvention articles, 2023-2024.

Phoenix Insights & Ipsos. "Career Advice for Longer Lives." Press release, May 18, 2023. https://www.thephoenixgroup.com/news-and-media/news-releases/2023/18-05-2023.

"PRESS RELEASE: Virgin Atlantic Becomes First Airline to Launch AI Champion Apprenticeship with Cambridge Spark." Cambridge Spark, March 26, 2025. https://www.cambridgespark.com/news/virgin-atlantic-first-in-industry-to-launch-ai-champion-apprenticeship-in-partnership-with-cambridge-spark.

Psychology Today. "Emotional Intelligence Test." Accessed July 2025. https://www.psychologytoday.com/us/tests/personality/emotional-intelligence-test.

Psychology Today. "The Psychology of Career Reinvention." November 2024.

PwC. "2024 AI Jobs Barometer." 2024. https://www.pwc.com/hu/hu/sajtoszoba/assets/ai_jobs_barometer_2024.pdf.

Recruiting industry newsletter on hiring trends, 2025.

Recruiter survey on in-demand skills. As cited in HR and recruiting industry reports, 2025.

Reddit user story. As cited in various online forums and articles on AI and career development, 2024.

"Resilience Test." Psychology Today, n.d. https://www.psychologytoday.com/us/tests/personality/resilience-test.

ResumeBuilder.com. "9 in 10 companies hiring want workers with ChatGPT experience." April 2023. https://www.resumebuilder.com/9-in-10-companies-hiring-want-workers-with-chatgpt-experience/.

Rijal, Hatim. Mastering ChatGPT for Job Search, Cover Letter & CV. Gumroad. https://hatimrijal.gumroad.com.

Rosenbaum, M. "The Great Career Reinvention, and How Workers Can Keep Up." Work Shift, May 20, 2025. https://workshift.org/the-great-career-reinvention/.

Saini, Kaustubh, Jaya Muvania, and Kaivan Dave. "AI Is Replacing Jobs in 2025: See Which Roles Are Disappearing." FinalRound AI, 2025. https://www.finalroundai.com/blog/ai-replacing-jobs-2025.

SHRM (Society for Human Resource Management). Research and reports on hiring technology, 2024.

Skilled Trades Report. As cited in various 2024 industry analyses on workforce trends.

"Small Businesses Leverage Generative AI for Growth and Productivity." AWIS, 2025. https://awis.org/ai-news/small-businesses-leverage-generative-ai-for-growth-and-productivity/.

Smith, Robert F. "Vista CEO Warns AI Will Eliminate 60% of Finance Jobs Among Attendees." Entrepreneur, June 5, 2025. https://www.entrepreneur.com/business-news/vista-ceo-tells-superreturn-attendees-ai-will-take-your-job/492825.

Sokolowski, Dmitry, Patrick Smith, et al. "High-Demand Human Skills In The Ongoing Age Of AI." Forbes, June 27, 2024. https://www.forbes.com/councils/forbestechcouncil/2024/06/27/high-demand-human-skills-in-the-ongoing-age-of-ai/.

Story of Kye and CoverDoc.ai. As circulated in tech and entrepreneurship forums, 2023-2024.

Study on junior employee productivity with AI assistants. As cited in technology and business publications, 2024.

Su, Jeff. 130+ ChatGPT Prompts for Job Seekers. Gumroad. https://jeffsu.gumroad.com/l/chatgpt-job-search-prompts.

Survey on tradespeople and AI. As cited in 2024 workforce and automation reports.

Swyx & Alessio. Latent Space. Podcast and Newsletter. https://www.latent.space.

Tamayo, J. et al. "Reskilling in the Age of AI." Harvard Business Review, September-October 2023.

Taylor, A. "The Wisdom Advantage: Thriving in Tech After 50." Medium, November 8, 2023.

Tegze, Jan. Ultimate Guide to ChatGPT for Job Seekers. Gumroad. https://jantegze.gumroad.com/l/ultimate-guide-chatgpt.

Tossell, Ben. Ben's Bites. Newsletter. https://bensbites.co.

Udacity. AI Product Manager Nanodegree. Online Program. https://www.udacity.com/course/ai-product-manager-nanodegree--nd088.

U.S. Bureau of Labor Statistics. Occupational Outlook Handbook. "Nurse Anesthetists, Nurse Midwives, and Nurse Practitioners." Updated September 2023. https://www.bls.gov/ooh/healthcare/nurse-anesthetists-nurse-midwives-and-nurse-practitioners.htm.

U.S. Bureau of Labor Statistics. Occupational Outlook Handbook. "Substance Abuse, Behavioral Disorder, and Mental Health Counselors." Updated September 2023. https://www.bls.gov/ooh/community-and-social-service/substance-abuse-behavioral-disorder-and-mental-health-counselors.htm.

Velasquez, Ignacio. 2,500+ ChatGPT Prompt Templates. Notion. https://ignacio-velasquez.notion.site/2-500-ChatGPT-Prompt-Templates-for-every-workflow-da15915a52254772963f4a39f4235859.

"Vibe Coding and AI Agents Resources." Zapier Blog. https://zapier.com/blog/ai-workflows-at-zapier.

Walmart. "Creating Opportunity for All American Workers." Corporate news release, April 7, 2025. https://corporate.walmart.com/news/2025/04/07/creating-opportunity-for-all-american-workers.

"When do you think we'll start to see serious job displacement from AI?" Reddit post. r/singularity, 2024. https://www.reddit.com/r/singularity/comments/1hilrs8/when_do_you_think_well_start_to_see_serious_job/.

Whittemore, Nathaniel. The AI Daily Brief (Formerly The AI Breakdown): Artificial Intelligence News and Analysis. Podcast. Accessed July 26, 2025. https://pod.link/1680633614.

"Why a Skills-First Approach Is the Future of Hiring." Inc.com, 2024.

"Why AI is making soft skills a top priority for HR." HR Executive, 2024. https://hrexecutive.com/why-ai-is-making-soft-skills-a-top-priority-for-hr/.

Wilson, Jordan. Everyday AI. Podcast.
https://www.youreverydayai.com.
Workday & Gallup. The State of AI at Work. 2024.
https://www.workday.com/en-us/resources/reports/the-state-of-ai-at-work.html.
World Economic Forum. "The Future of Jobs Report 2023."
April 2023.
https://www.weforum.org/publications/the-future-of-jobs-report-2023/.
Zapier. Company case studies and marketing materials, 2024.
Zhang, Michael, et al. "What Workers Really Want from Artificial Intelligence." Stanford University Human-Centered Artificial Intelligence (HAI), 2024.
https://hai.stanford.edu/news/what-workers-really-want-artificial-intelligence.
Zippia. "25+ Overwhelming Recruiting Statistics." 2024.
https://www.zippia.com/advice/recruiting-statistics/.

About the Author

Ryan Brooks is an engineer, product developer and strategist focused on the intersection of artificial intelligence and the workplace. With a deep understanding of both the technical and business implications of AI, he is dedicated to helping professionals navigate the complexities of their career.

Ryan holds specializations in Generative AI in Business from the University of Michigan and Generative AI Leadership from Vanderbilt University. His passion for real-world business applications of AI drives his continuous research to keep up with the fast pace of new developments.

His background, which includes an MBA and a degree in chemical engineering, provides him with a unique, analytical lens to empower professionals with the strategic mindsets needed to build resilient careers.

***

Thank you for reading Future-Proof. If you found this guide helpful, please consider leaving a review on Amazon. Your feedback makes a real difference in helping other professionals discover this book and navigate their own careers.

www.ingramcontent.com/pod-product-compliance
Lightning Source LLC
Chambersburg PA
CBHW071548210326
41597CB00019B/3156